WHAT MAKES A MATILDA

PUFFIN BOOKS

UK | USA | Canada | Ireland | Australia
India | New Zealand | South Africa | China

Penguin Random House Australia is part of the Penguin Random House group of companies whose addresses can be found at global.penguinrandomhouse.com.

First published by Puffin Books, an imprint of Penguin Random House Australia Pty Ltd, in 2022

Cover photographs, all via Getty Images: team Matt King/Getty Images Sport; Mary Fowler and Sam Kerr Steve Christo/Corbis Sport; Clare Polkinghorne Cameron Spencer/Getty Images Sport; Caitlin Foord and Ellie Carpenter Mark Kolbe/Getty Images Sport

Internal photographs: Latrobe Ladies' Football Club, 1921 photographs, John Oxley Library, State Library of Queensland; all other photographs © Football Australia.

Internal images: © mhatzapa/Shutterstock.com, © Tiwat K/Shutterstock.com, © balabolka/Shutterstock.com, © Natasha Pankina/Shutterstock.com, © JosepPerianes/Shutterstock.com, © Dmytro Nychytalyuk/Shutterstock.com, © JJ Chamon/Shutterstock.com, © Prokhorovich/Shutterstock.com, © Nikolaeva/Shutterstock.com, © KUCO/Shutterstock.com, © Ola_view/Shutterstock.com, © alongzo/Shutterstock.com, © VasilkovS/Shutterstock.com, © Kanate/Shutterstock.com, © primiaou/Shutterstock.com, © Cube29/Shutterstock.com

Design by Caroline Lee © Penguin Random House Australia Pty Ltd

Printed and bound in Australia by Griffin Press, an accredited ISO AS/NZS 14001 Environmental Management Systems printer

Penguin Random House Australia uses papers that are natural and recyclable products, made from wood grown in sustainable forests. The logging and manufacture processes are expected to conform to the environmental regulations of the country of origin.

A catalogue record for this book is available from the National Library of Australia

ISBN 978 1 76 104886 9 (Paperback)

penguin.com.au

We at Penguin Random House Australia acknowledge that Aboriginal and Torres Strait Islander peoples are the Traditional Custodians and the first storytellers of the lands on which we live and work. We honour Aboriginal and Torres Strait Islander peoples' continuous connection to Country, waters, skies and communities. We celebrate Aboriginal and Torres Strait Islander stories, traditions and living cultures; and we pay our respects to Elders past and present.

WHAT MAKES A MATILDA

CommBank MATILDAS

Player Stories, Tips, Advice, Football Drills and So Much More!

PUFFIN BOOKS

Women's football in Australia - the beginning

Looking at how much Australia loves the Matildas, it's easy to imagine that they've been one of Australia's most loved and well-known sporting teams forever, but it hasn't always been this way. The success and fame of the Matildas has been built on decades of women fighting the odds and working really hard to play great football in and for Australia.

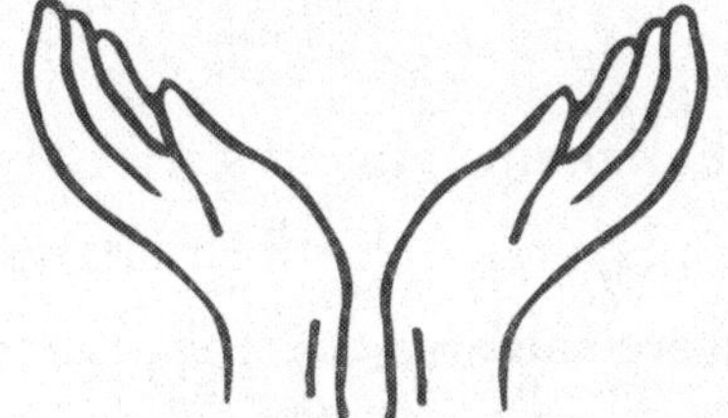

The idea of kicking a ball around for sport is thousands of years old, so it wasn't exactly new when people started choosing the rules that define football as we know it today. The way we now play the game (from club matches all the way to the World Cup) is technically called association football, and was refined by men in England, over more than twenty years, culminating in the very first FA Cup in 1872.

Association football made its way to Australia in the 1870s. One of the first women's teams played in 1903, when a delegation of women employed by the Clyde Engineering Sports Club convinced the company to support them. The women wore repurposed cycling wear for training. Other teams formed in Candelo in 1908 and in 1916 in West Wallsend, both in New South Wales, and two girls' teams played a High School match in Toowoomba, Queensland in 1917. By the 1920s, more and more women around Australia wanted to play with, and against, other women, so they started to take charge and form women-only football teams and clubs.

Over 100 women formed the Queensland Ladies' Soccer Football Association in July 1921. These women loved football and enthusiastically campaigned to form their own league. They wanted an official competition all of their own! The Latrobe Ladies was one of the first women's football clubs to ever exist in Australia, and over 100 years later, they have a women's team called Bardon Latrobe today. Women's football associations were popping up around the country, and teams were playing regularly (albeit unofficially).

Then, in September 1921, two women's football teams played a friendly match on the Brisbane Cricket Ground. The players of North Brisbane (the Reds) and South Brisbane (the Blues) were selected from the three strongest teams playing in Brisbane at the time. This would be the first representative women's football match in Australian history. The women were very proud to represent their city.

The teams walked onto the pitch to rousing cheers, and then the game was underway. The Reds took an early lead, attacking hard and fast to attempt their first goal in the opening minutes of the game. The Blues' goalkeeper saved the shot, but the play – and the support of the crowd – had given the Reds an unbeatable energy. The Blues fought hard. They just couldn't stop the Reds scoring in the first half. Both teams were more confident in the second half, but a fatal error by the Blues awarded the Reds a penalty kick, and Jean Campbell scored. Jean was so good the crowd cheered her name, 'Jean! Jean! Jean!'. The Blues tried and tried but couldn't score and the Reds won 2–0.

The match had been widely advertised as an exhibition between two men's games. More than 10,000 people turned up to watch the women's teams show off their skills and cheer them on to victory. Wondering how that compares to today's crowds? The average attendance for the 2018–19 men's A League (the most recent season not affected by the pandemic) was 10,877.

It took almost three months to go from the first association and practice on the training ground to that famous Brisbane match in 1921. By that time, English women's teams were touring around England playing in front of huge crowds – record-breaking crowds – raising money for charity and supporting other women who wanted to play. It was about time the Aussies caught up!

Three weeks after the first game, the Reds and Blues headlined their own match. This time in a town called Ipswich.

Even without a men's game after, over 3000 people turned up to watch the women play a fiercely competitive match that ended in a 2-2 draw. It was clear that women's football was here to stay!

But then, just two months later, disturbing news came from England. The English Football Association had decided that football wasn't suitable for women and banned its clubs from letting women's teams play on their grounds or use their referees. The ban didn't apply to Australian clubs, but a lot of Australian football officials looked to England for guidance. In 1922, an Australian committee recommended that football was an unsuitable sport for women to play as it was too demanding on their health.

This was devastating for the growth of the women's game in Australia. Women became scared of what people would think of them if they played, and even if they *did* still play, opportunities for games were drying up fast. Any matches that did occur were mostly played in private, and deliberately went unpublicised until *after* they'd happened. It was a completely different atmosphere to the year before.

Many players tried to get football matches going again. Teams formed in Newcastle and Illawarra (1928–1933), in Broken Hill (1936) and Sydney (1942–1943), in Rockhampton (1946) and many other towns around the country. Without resources, and with the lack of official support and tournaments, it was really difficult to keep it going. The development of women's football stalled until the 1960s. In 1970s, the English Football Association finally reversed their ban and people started to be more open to the idea of women playing the sport.

It may have taken a while for women's football to regain popularity in Australia, but when it did, they really made up for lost time! In 1974 - more than fifty years after the Brisbane matches - a national women's football competition was established.

This was a *huge* step in acknowledging women's football as a valid sport in Australia. Not only were there official matches for the teams to play, but now they finally had organised leagues of their own.

In August 1974, five women's teams from four states came together for the first National Women's Soccer Championships in Sydney. And at the end of the competition, something very important happened: team officials got together and agreed to establish the Australian Women's Soccer Association to ensure that women's football would continue to grow and develop, just like the women who met in Brisbane all those years ago had hoped. It's fair to say they achieved what they'd set out to do! Within eleven years the senior Championships had expanded to include nine states/territories along with Junior and Youth divisions. Today, Australia's female footballers are some of the best-known players in the world.

YOU GOTTA AIM HIGH

CORTNEE VINE

Women's football on the world stage

Even in the 1970s, when women finally had their own national football competition, it was really difficult for them to be taken seriously. High-level footballers had to contribute to their teams financially just to be able to train and play, including buying their own uniforms and paying for their own travel to national championships and competitions. They also often had to take time off their actual jobs in order to meet team commitments.

As if this didn't make it hard enough, they also suffered ridicule while they trained and played. People would come to watch the women practise, but instead of calling encouragement they would heckle and yell insults. Women playing football competitively were viewed as oddities at best, though the newspapers called them far worse. The English Football Association's fifty-year ban had tarnished the women's game worldwide – even in

England, where women's matches had previously been so popular they'd set attendance records that stood until the 2012 London Olympics. Instead, women playing football had largely been reduced to nothing more than something to gawk at.

Australia's female footballers didn't give up though. The public would come around eventually, and, in the meantime, they were going to keep training and playing games in Australia and internationally. They weren't completely without supporters, either. Many people associated with the men's game believed in the development of the women's game too.

In 1975, just a year after the first National Championships, a Sydney based club team (named for the tournament as Australian XI) competed in the inaugural Asian Women's Championship – the precursor for the AFC Asian Women's Cup. It was the first internationally sanctioned tournament Australian women had played in!

The team had to undertake months of fundraising to afford to travel to the tournament in Hong Kong. Once there, they played well enough across their four matches to finish second in their group stage and ultimately place third overall! The overall event was an incredible experience for the team, who played in front of thousands of fans.

Then, in 1978, Australia was invited to participate in the World Women's Invitational Tournament in Taiwan. It was a big deal. Teams from thirteen countries would be attending, and the tournament organisers would pay some of the costs for travel and accommodation.

The Australian Women's Soccer Association rose to the occasion by appointing the first national coach to select players from across the country to represent the best of what we had to offer (including four players from Australian XI). This was the birth of Australia's national women's team. It still wasn't regarded as our first true international competition though because many of the other countries fielded club teams rather than national teams, which weren't created until some years later.

Luckily, the national team didn't have to wait very long before they were able to compete in their first ever 'A' international – a match against another national team selected from the best players another country has to offer.

In October 1979, New Zealand sent its own nationally selected team to Australia to play in three test matches. The first game in Sydney was hard-fought, ending in a 2–2 draw, just like that first Brisbane match six decades earlier. Julie Dolan, who had played in both the Asian Women's Championship and the World Women's Invitational Tournament, was Australia's captain for the match and holds the number one cap for the women's national team.

Players on the national team receive actual caps for debut appearances and for milestones. The cap signifies that a footballer has played for the national team in senior A-international games against other national teams. Some players have more than one hundred caps for the Matildas (that's the number of games they've played, not actual hats!).

Australia and New Zealand met twice more in the three-match series, with the games ending 1–0 to New Zealand, then 1–0 to Australia in Brisbane for an overall series draw.

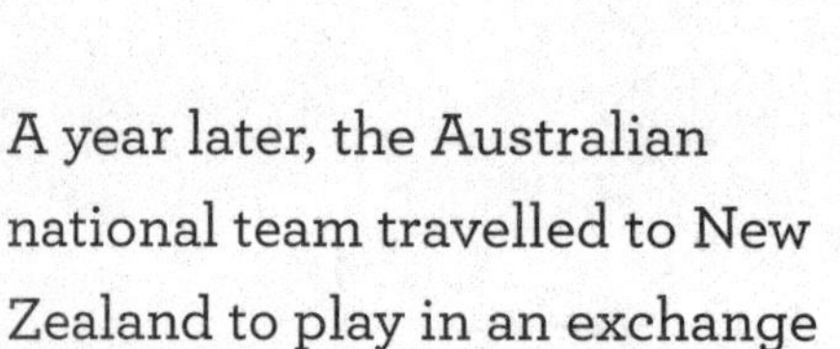

A year later, the Australian national team travelled to New Zealand to play in an exchange series. They drew the first match 3–3, finished the second game 1–1 and finally won the decider 3–2 after Sandra Brentnall scored a hat-trick. In fact, Brentnall scored in all three games!

The two teams played against each other again in 1981 in New Zealand with Australia securing a 2–1 win. Then, in 1983, Australia, New Zealand, New Caledonia and Fiji formed the Oceania Women's Football Confederation and started playing in tournaments every three years. Teams from Chinese Taipei (from 1986) and Papua New Guinea (from 1989) also participated as time went on.

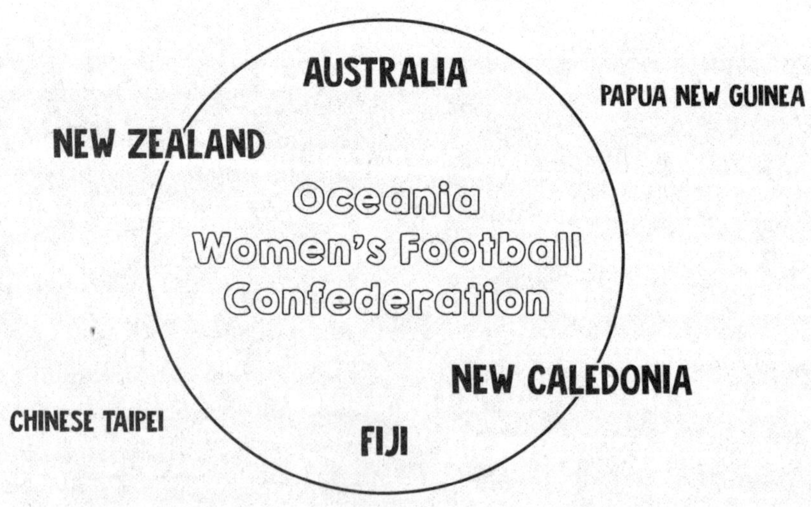

The Australian team was well and truly cemented as a vital part of women's football in Australia and the Oceania region, proving to the world that the women's game was here to stay.

And, in 2022, the first ever football team of Aussie women to play an international tournament – the 1975 Australian XI squad – were officially recognised as Matildas, forty-seven years after they played in Hong Kong.

The ParaMatildas

When the national team competed in the 1988 FIFA Women's Invitational tournament, they were part of international women's football history. Almost thirty-five years later, the ParaMatildas – a brand new team launched by Football Australia in 2022 – became part of an equally historical event: the very first IFCPF Women's World Cup (that's the International Federation of CP Football, who are the organisation responsible for governing CP football across the globe).

The ParaMatildas play CP football. CP stands for cerebral palsy, which is a health condition that affects movement, reflexes, posture and muscle tone. In a women's CP football game, each team fields five players across two halves of thirty minutes each. The pitch is smaller too, and some of the rules are different.

More than 2.2 million women and girls live with disability in Australia. The ParaMatildas are playing an integral part in raising the visibility of CP football, and showing women and girls with

cerebral palsy, acquired brain injury and symptoms of stroke that there are opportunities for athletes with disability to compete on the international stage.

The team is an inspiration for the next generation, showing passion, resilience and a 'Never Say Die' attitude (like the Matildas). They also make a difference as role models for everyone from kids to their coaches. Head coach Kelly Stirton has been working to create pathways for athletes with disability for years through grassroots and community programs, and even now the ParaMatildas players still teach her new things. She says the passion they bring to the game is infectious.

It took a lot of years of hard work and commitment for the ParaMatildas team to launch. In fact, they're the first new senior national Australian football team to be announced in twenty-two years! The Pararoos (the men's CP football team) was founded in 1998 – just in time to compete in the Sydney 2000 Paralympics.

CP football has been a Paralympic sport with regular World Cup tournaments since 1984, but it's always been a men's event – no women's teams have ever competed. Until 2022, there had never been any international women's CP football tournaments at all. This actually made the International Paralympic Committee decide to not allow men's CP events in the next Paralympics, and maybe not the ones that follow, until they did something about it.

To address the imbalance and make CP football more inclusive, the IFCPF planned the first CP Women's World Cup. In May 2022, five women's teams – including the ParaMatildas – came together in Salou, Spain to play on the international stage.

Getting to Spain was a community effort for the ParaMatildas. The team raised funds through initiatives like the Undefeated Giving Day in April, and was one of five charities heroed in the PFA's (Professional Footballers Australia) 'Play it Forward' campaign, which aimed to fundraise and support, community and football initiatives. Thanks to a swell of support from the Australian public, the team was able to fund their World Cup campaign. It was time to play CP football on the world stage!

The ParaMatildas flew to Spain wanting to do well in the tournament, of course, but more importantly, they wanted to enjoy their football. And enjoy it they did!

The ParaMatildas headed into the tournament ranked fourth in the world. They played five matches across six days, facing each team at the group stage before they went head-to-head with the team from the USA to see who would take out the final!

Up first though was Australia's history-making match against the Netherlands in the group stage. The ParaMatildas played strongly from kick off, with a starting five of Tahlia Blanshard, Lainee Harrison, Katelyn Smith (GK), Eloise Northam (C) and Georgia Beikoff. Beikoff scored the ParaMatildas first-ever international goal at three minutes, with another six goals scored by Australia (including two more by Beikoff and a long throw by Northam) to finish the first half leading by seven. Nicole Christodoulou, Charlize Tran and Matilda Mason were subbed in during the second half, and the team held onto their lead thanks to five more goals and fantastic goal-keeping by Katelyn Smith to end the match at 12–0.

Two days later, the ParaMatildas faced Japan in their second match. The ParaMatildas' starting five was the same as for their first match, but this time Beikoff was the captain. It was also her birthday! The match was a tight game from the start. The Japanese team mounted a strong defence, but Eloise Northam eventually broke the stalemate with Australia's first goal. Two more goals followed and the ParaMatildas closed out the first half up 3–0. In the second half, Australia scored another goal and Rae Anderson was subbed in for her debut. The game finished at 4–0 with Australia starting to look like they were headed to the final!

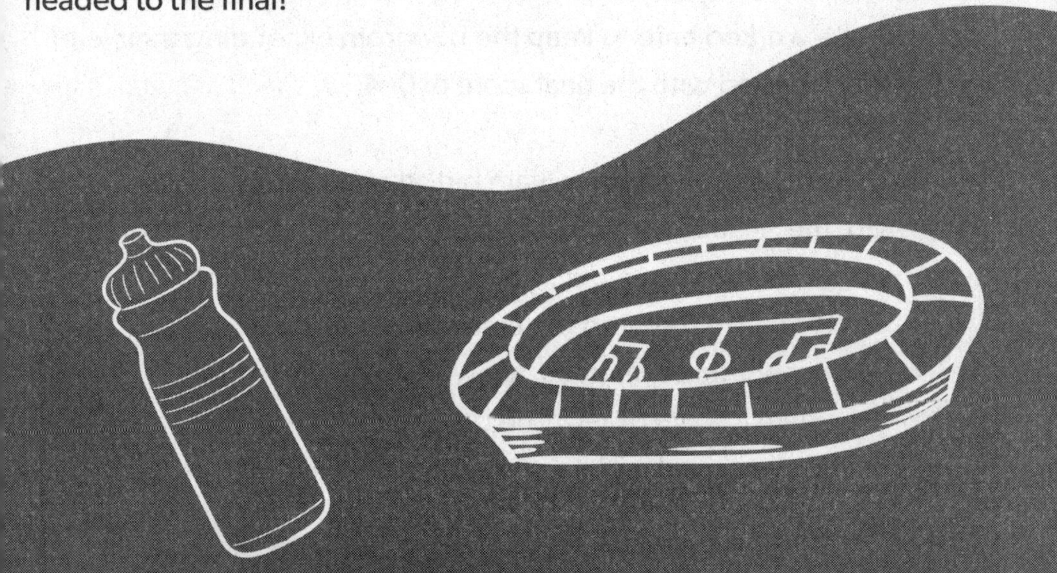

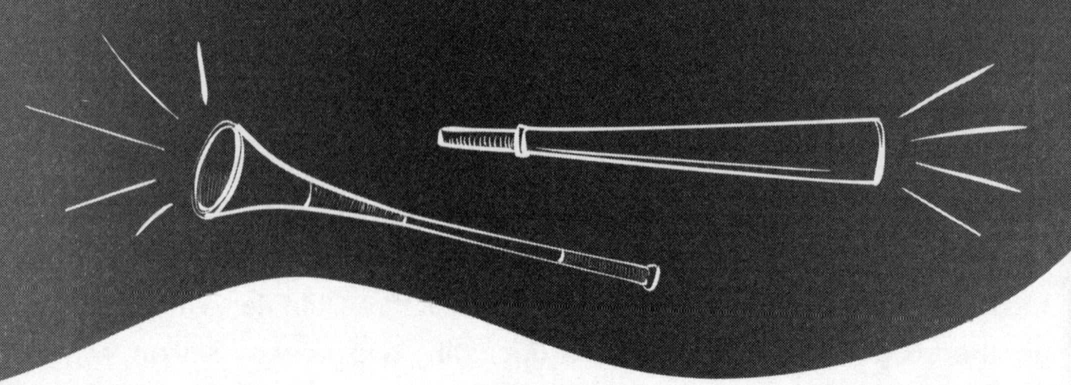

Australia versus Spain was the third match, with the same winning starting line-up as the previous matches. Goals came quickly in this game, with Beikoff scoring the first goal in the first minute – the quickest goal of the entire tournament. Anderson and Holly Saunders were subbed in during the first half, and the team had a 7–0 lead going into the break. The ParaMatildas played beautifully in the second half, with Christodoulou and Mason subbing in to help Australia close the game at 11–0.

By the time the ParaMatildas headed into their fourth match, they knew they were going to be playing in the final against the very team they were about to face: the USA. The starting five this time was Beikoff (C), Smith (GK), Blanshard, Harrison and Anderson, with Tran, Northam and Christodoulou subbing in throughout the match. The score stayed at nil-all until close to half-time, when the USA team scored three goals. Katelyn Smith worked hard to keep the USA from expanding their lead, and the game ended with the final score of 0–4.

Three days later (and on another team birthday – this time for Tahlia Blanshard!), the Australian and USA teams took the field again for the final. The ParaMatildas came out strong with their original starting five. Eloise Northam (C) scored the first goal of the match after a hard-fought twenty-three minutes, allowing Australia to head into half-time with a score of 1–0. The USA team evened the score in the thirty-second minute, then scored a second goal moments later, pushing them ahead. As the game went into extra time, the ParaMatildas managed another goal, but couldn't equal the USA team's score, and the match closed at 4–2. After an amazing tournament, the ParaMatildas finished as proud silver medallists.

The ParaMatildas' accolades didn't end with their silver medal, either. The IFCPF honoured two of the team members at the end of the tournament. Georgia Beikoff was awarded the 2022 IFCPF Women's World Cup Golden Boot, and Katelyn Smith was named 2022 IFCPF Women's World Cup Best Goalkeeper!

The tournament was a historic event, and the ParaMatildas were thrilled to win silver and climb the rankings to become the world number one nation. The 2022 IFCPF Women's World Cup was just the start of their story – there's so much more to come!

Meet the

2022 IFCPF Women's World Cup Team

GOALKEEPERS

Holly Saunders

- Jersey #1
- Age: 19
- From: Sydney, NSW
- Played one game, debuting against Spain
- Holly is no stranger to sport on the international stage – she's the current T35 Long Jump World Record holder!

Katelyn Smith

- Jersey #6
- Age: 26
- From: Perth, WA
- Played all five games, debuting against the Netherlands
- Scored two goals
- Awarded 2022 IFCPF Women's World Cup Best Goalkeeper

"As a little girl growing up, I wanted to be a Matilda. Knowing that there is a ParaMatildas pathway now too is even better. To be in the very first [ParaMatildas] team is just the icing on the cake."

FORWARDS

Nicole Christodoulou

- Jersey #2
- Age: 30
- From: Sydney, NSW
- Played three games, debuting against the Netherlands
- Scored two goals

"We're going to make all of you proud."

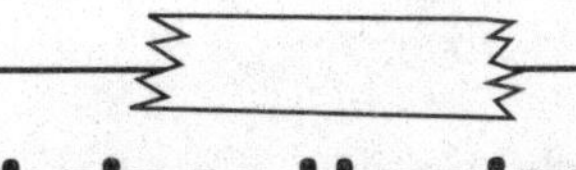

Lainee Harrison

- Jersey #5
- Age: 18
- From: Newcastle, NSW
- Played all five games, debuting against the Netherlands
- Scored five goals

Charlize Tran

- Jersey #4
- Age: 15
- From: Sydney, NSW
- Played three games, debuting against the Netherlands
- Scored one goal
- Charlize was the youngest player selected for the national team.

Rae Anderson

- Jersey #9
- Age: 25
- From: Wamberal, NSW
- Played three games, debuting against Japan
- Rae Anderson has represented Australia in both the summer and the winter Paralympics in discus and javelin at the summer games, and alpine skiing and slalom in the winter games!

"I've always dreamed of having a sporting career."

MIDFIELDERS

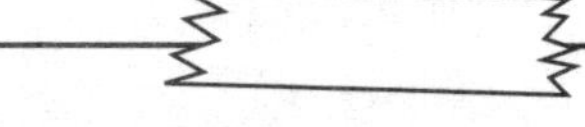

Eloise Northam – co-captain

- Jersey #7
- Age: 19
- From: Sydney, NSW
- Played all five games, debuting against the Netherlands
- Scored 5 goals

Georgia Beikoff – co-captain

- Jersey #10
- Age: 29
- From: Newcastle, NSW
- Played all five games, debuting against the Netherlands
- Scored 13 goals
- Awarded 2022 IFCPF Women's World Cup Golden Boot
- Like Rae Anderson, Georgia Beikoff is also a Paralympian. She won bronze in the F37/38 javelin at the 2012 London Paralympics as well as competing in the 4x100m relay.
- She's been playing football since she was six, and said that playing for the ParaMatildas was a dream come true.

"Just because we have limitations, it doesn't stop us from doing what we love."

DEFENDERS

Tahlia Blanshard

- Jersey #3
- Age: 21
- From: Jilliby, NSW
- Played all five games, debuting against the Netherlands

"This is about making sure that every single person feels included and accepted because feeling that sense of belonging is the most beautiful thing in the whole world."

Matilda Mason

- Jersey #8
- Age: 30
- From: Canberra, ACT
- Played two games, debuting against the Matildas

"This is our chance to shine and show Australia and the world that women and girls with a disability deserve the chance to live their full dreams."

HEAD COACH

Kelly Stirton

→ Stirton is an all-abilities coach who has been advocating for diversity in football opportunities for a long time.

"This team will stand proudly alongside their Commonwealth Bank Matildas teammates as iconic female footballers and that is an incredible visual that we are portraying as a sport."

Stories and Advice from the ParaMatildas

What is the best moment of your career so far?

Captaining the ParaMatildas at our very first World Cup was very special. Although, there are a few other moments, like scoring the first ever goal and receiving the Golden Boot.

- Georgia Beikoff

What's the best thing about being a ParaMatilda?

The best thing about being a ParaMatilda is having the opportunity to wear the Australian crest over my heart. It's a very surreal and emotional feeling that not many people get to experience, so I appreciate every single second of it!

- Nicole Christodoulou

The birth of the Matildas

In 1988, after years of countries creating their own international women's football competitions, FIFA (the international governing body for association football) finally decided to test the waters and see if there was enough global interest in the women's game to hold a World Cup. In contrast, male footballers had had access to international tournaments since FIFA was founded in 1904, and an official World Cup since 1930.

1988

The FIFA Women's Invitational tournament (often referred to as the Pilot World Cup) was held in China over twelve days in June 1988. Twelve nationally selected teams representing Australia, Brazil, Canada, China PR, Czechoslovakia, Ivory Coast, Japan, Netherlands, Norway, Sweden, Thailand and the United States came together to compete. It wasn't quite a World Cup, but it was the last step on the way.

Australia played well in the group stage, winning the first game 1–0 against Brazil, when Janine Riddington scored Australia's first goal in a FIFA tournament. A win against Thailand and a loss to Norway was enough for the team to progress to the quarter-finals, where they were knocked out of the competition by China. Their elimination didn't dim their success though – by playing in the tournament, the team helped make history for women's football in Australia and around the globe.

Upwards of 15,000 fans watched each match of the tournament, with crowds increasing at each stage. The final, between Sweden and Norway, was attended by over 30,000 fans (which was more than some of the matches in the men's World Cup two years earlier!), proving that people really were passionate about women's football.

It was enough for FIFA as the 1988 event was determined a great success, and planning began for a Women's World Championship to be held once again in China in 1991. The Australian team didn't qualify for that first tournament as old rivals New Zealand won the Oceania qualification tournament on goal difference, but Australia did qualify for the World Cup four years later in Sweden, and they haven't missed a single one of the World Cups that have been held every four years since (with FIFA retrospectively deeming the 1991 championship as 'the 1st Women's World Cup').

The Matildas

With the introduction of the FIFA Women's World Cup™, interest in the women's national team began to pick up. When the team qualified for the second World Cup in 1995, the Australian Women's Soccer Association (AWSA) capitalised on public interest to give the team its very own nickname. Up until then, people had been calling them various names such as the Female Socceroos and the Soccerbelles!

The AWSA partnered with the SBS television network to run a competition to settle on a nickname for the women's national team. The options were narrowed down and then a top-five shortlist was broadcast, with viewers voting for their favourite name.

At the end of the polling, the other shortlisted names (the Soccertoos, the Blue Flyers, the Waratahs and the Lorikeets) were knocked off, and our national team gained their official nickname:

THE MATILDAS

It was a promising time for women's football. Following worldwide lobbying led by officials from Australia and supporters of the USA national women's team, the sport was going to become a staple of the Olympic Games (to be debuted in the 1996 Atlanta Games), the Australian Women's Soccer Association had started to receive greater levels of government funding and, for the first time, Australia's national team was able to afford a full-time coach.

1995

The Matildas had a tough introduction to their first World Cup in Sweden. They faced Denmark, China PR and the United States in their group rounds and unfortunately lost each game. They managed to score three goals across the three matches, which was a first for *any* Australian football team. The Socceroos had qualified for one World Cup at this point, but hadn't scored any goals during the tournament. So when Angela Iannotta scored against China in the Matildas' second FIFA Women's World Cup game, it was a historic moment for Australian football.

1999

When the Matildas went to the next World Cup in the USA in 1999, with an increase from twelve to sixteen teams, they faced Ghana, Sweden and China PR in the group rounds, drawing the first match and losing the other two, resulting in another elimination at the group stage.

The Matildas placed higher in the overall tournament ranking than they had in 1995 though, and were starting to see just how much the world cared about women's football – crowds for the FIFA Women's World Cup 1999™ were ten times what they'd been in 1995 with the final between China and host nation USA played before a sell out crowd of 90,185! As an extra silver lining for Australia: up next was the 2000 Sydney Olympics – which the Matildas had automatically qualified for as the host country. They were set to play an international tournament on home soil. That's a story for later though. Read about the Matildas at the Olympics on page 122.

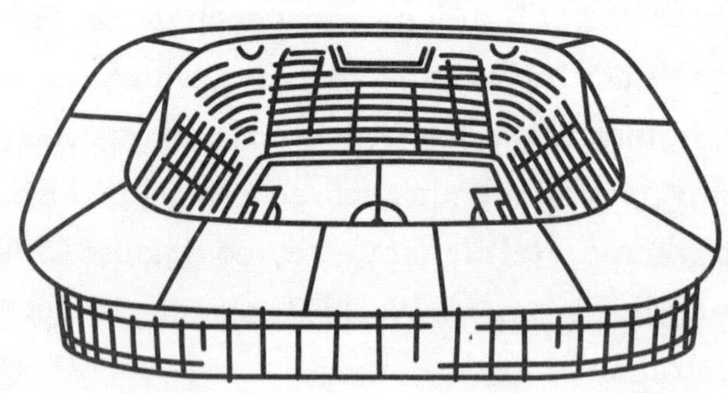

2003

The next World Cup was held again in the USA, in 2003, with the Matildas facing Russia, China PR and Ghana in their group stage. Despite Australia scoring first in their first two matches, they ultimately lost all three.

The Matildas had been eliminated at the group stage, but their progress on the international field was clear. They were consistently qualifying for the World Cup, and over the three tournaments their goal difference (the number of goals a team scored minus the number of goals other teams scored against them) had shrunk from minus ten to minus two. It was a fantastic indicator of how much the team had improved, and how far they'd come.

When FIFA released their very first international ranking of women's football teams, the Matildas came in close to the top at number fifteen (out of 108).

SPOTLIGHT

Clare Polkinghorne

DOB
1 February 1989

Brisbane, Queensland

4

SENIOR DEBUT

Queensland Roar (now Brisbane Roar) 2008

MATILDAS DEBUT

Australia vs China, China tour
June 2006, aged 17

Clare Polkinghorne has had the kind of career a professional player dreams of: she's one of the Matildas' most-capped players ever, was the first female footballer to play one hundred games in the W-League and has played for several clubs across multiple countries and continents. And at thirty-three, with more than sixteen years of professional football under her belt, she's still going strong.

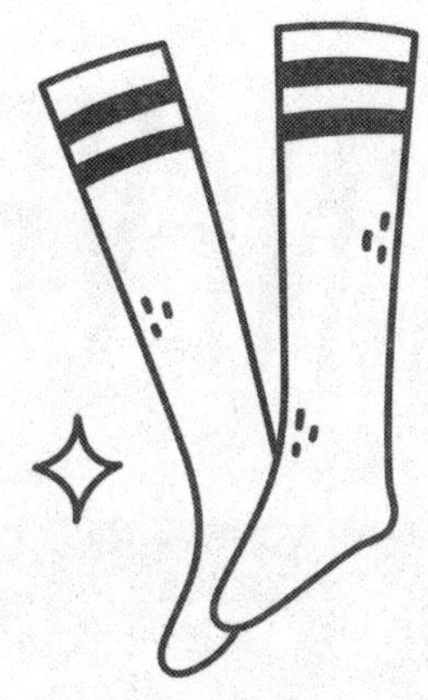

Incredibly, until she ended her time with Brisbane Roar in 2021, Clare had also played every single season of the W-League since it was established in 2008 – and all for the same club! Because the W-League wasn't established until 2008, Clare actually made her Matildas debut before she ever played a senior league match for Brisbane.

Clare now plays in the Swedish league for Vittsjö GIK, where she's signed until at least 2023. The longevity of her career comes down to her professional attitude and her continual desire to develop her skills as one of the world's best defenders.

'NEVER SAY DIE'

'Never Say Die' has been the Matildas' motto since 2007, coined during their breakthrough campaign at that year's World Cup in China. In fact, it's so much a part of the team's ethos that it's stitched into the back of their jerseys. The team is known worldwide for their 'Never Say Die' spirit.

'Never Say Die' means never giving up. It means persevering against the biggest odds and always believing that you can come back from behind.

The Matildas have tapped into this attitude from the team's earliest days, when they trained and played despite adversity and everything thrown at them – the insults, the lack of decent facilities, the rarity of international tournaments. It's what led them to be a part of the movement to give women footballers their own World Cup, and why there's a Matildas team today.

It's also in the way that so many of the current generation of Matildas persevered despite the lack of girls' teams at the club level, playing with the boys while the women's game grew up around them. It's in the sacrifices they've made to make their mark on the footballing community at home and internationally.

It's a motto that's served them well in times of injury and illness – a reminder that sprained joints and torn muscles and even broken backs aren't necessarily the end of a professional football career. It's helped them think positive while they're undergoing rehab, thinking about what it will be like to finally step back on the pitch.

It's the guiding principle that sees them perform spectacularly on the field, becoming an internationally renowned team, continually improving on their past performances. It's what gives them the confidence to come back from behind and to overcome the worst conditions. With the 'Never Say Die' mentality, the Matildas can always play the game their way and be proud of what they've achieved – win or lose.

It's something they carry into every aspect of their lives too – about so much more than football. It's something they will never take for granted.

The 'Never Say Die' spirit is one of the most core parts of what makes a Matilda. With that kind of fighting spirit and belief, the team can do anything.

SPOTLIGHT

Emily van Egmond

DOB
12 July 1993

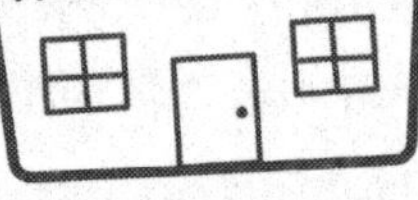

10

SENIOR DEBUT
Newcastle United Jets
2008

MATILDAS DEBUT
Australia vs Korea
friendly match
March 2010, aged 16

Emily van Egmond had an early introduction to the world of professional football – her dad is a former Socceroo and Newcastle United Jets coach! When her twin brother refused to wear his soccer uniform, Emily stepped up instead, taking her brother's place. She ended up playing on boys' soccer teams – coached by her dad, of course – until she was fifteen. That's when she first started playing at the senior club level.

Her first selection for the Matildas happened just a couple of years later, for a duo of friendlies against Italy. But then, disaster: she dislodged a bone in her ankle during training and was forced to sit out the matches. Two months later, she was finally able to make her international debut. Now, Emily has played more than 120 games for Australia. She was the eighth Matilda to play one hundred matches, and is one of the team's top goal scorers.

Like most of the senior team members, she's also played for clubs around the world. She's made it a priority not to leave her roots behind though – she still makes regular appearances for the Newcastle Jets.

The 2007 World Cup campaign

In 2006, the Australian Football Federation left the Oceania Football Confederation to join the more competitive Asian Football Confederation. The Matildas went from being the top-ranked team in the OFC to the fourth-ranked team in the AFC.

The move came just in time for Australia to host the AFC Women's Asian Cup in Adelaide. The cup was the qualifying competition for the FIFA Women's World Cup 2007™, and the Matildas were determined to win one of the coveted top two spots (only the two best teams of the tournament would qualify for the World Cup). The Matildas faced four teams in the group stage, winning 4–0 against South Korea, 2–0 against Myanmar, drawing 0–0 with North Korea and then winning 5–0 over

Thailand to move into the semi-final knockout. They faced Japan in the semis, with Caitlin Munoz scoring a goal in the first ten minutes. A goal by Joanne Peters in the forty-fifth minute cemented the Matildas' lead, and they were through to the final!

A nailbiting match between Australia and China PR ensued, with both Munoz and Peters scoring in the first half. China equalised in the second half, and the match went into kicks from the penalty spot.

A game only goes into a penalty shootout if it ends in a draw during the knockout stage of a tournament, which is why the Matildas didn't require penalty kicks in their group-stage draw with North Korea.

China scored four goals to the Matildas' two, and were declared the winners of the tournament, with Australia securing the runners up medals. The team was ecstatic as the top two teams of the Asian Cup were heading to the FIFA Women's World Cup 2007™. The Matildas had qualified once again!

In 2007, the World Cup was held in September in China. Sixteen teams from six confederations came together over three weeks to face off for the world championship title. The Matildas faced Ghana, Norway and Canada in their group, with a win against Ghana and a draw with Norway in the first two games.

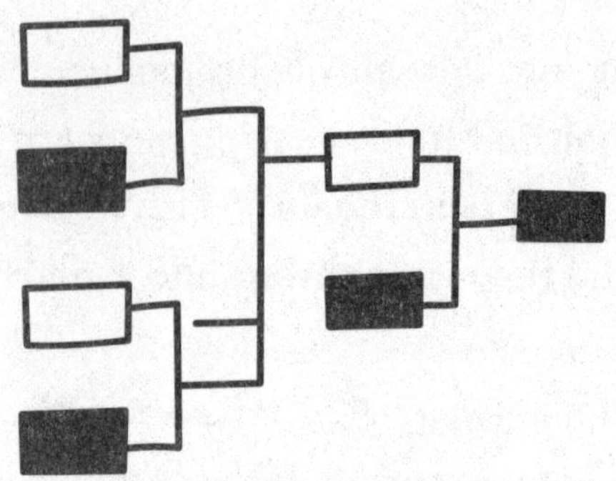

With Canada having lost to Norway earlier in the group, Australia had a golden opportunity: if they could win or draw against the Canadians, they would achieve something monumental for the team and advance out of the group stage.

It was an edge-of-your-seat match, and at first it seemed like the Matildas weren't going to make it. They were down 2–1 as the game headed into injury time and then, against all odds, captain Cheryl Salisbury (the most capped Australian player, male or female, with 151 games!) scored a last-minute equaliser in the ninety-second minute. For the very first time, the Matildas were heading to a World Cup quarter-final!

Australia faced Brazil in the knockout game in front of a crowd of 35,000 – one of the largest the team had ever experienced. The Matildas came back from 2–0 down with goals at the thirty-sixth and sixty-eighth minutes to equalise, but ultimately lost the match when Brazil sunk a goal in the seventy-fifth minute for a final score of 3–2.

Still, reaching the quarter-final was a fantastic result, and the Matildas ended the World Cup ranked sixth overall. Members of the team were named Player of the Match for three of Australia's four matches, and attacker Lisa De Vanna was named on the All-Star Team of the Tournament. FIFA praised the team's winning mentality, excellent team spirit and ability to stay focused after falling behind – the Matildas had made their mark on the international stage.

Unfortunately, women's football was still receiving a *lot* less attention than men's football. Across the world, it was considered largely a men's game and to watch women play was thought to be less interesting (at least by media companies and television networks, who were reluctant to buy into broadcast rights or other coverage). Less media attention unfortunately also meant less interest from sponsors and investors.

The Matildas were ranked twelfth in the world to the Australian men's team's (the Socceroos') rank of forty-eight, and outperformed the men's team in international tournaments, but they were still working at a disadvantage to receive the same funding, access to facilities, media support and public renown.

The FIFA Women's World Cup 2007™ squad

GOALKEEPERS

Melissa Barbieri
- Jersey #1
- Age: 27
- Home club: Victoria Vision

Lydia Williams
- Jersey #18
- Age: 19
- Home club: Canberra Eclipse

Emma Wirkus
- Jersey #21
- Age: 25
- Home club: Adelaide Sensation

DEFENDERS

Kate McShea
- » Jersey #2
- » Age: 24
- » Home club: Queensland Sting

Dianne Alagich
- » Jersey #4
- » Age: 28
- » Home club: NSW Sapphires

Cheryl Salisbury – captain
- » Jersey #5
- » Age: 33
- » Home club: Northern NSW Pride

Rhian Davies
- » Jersey #6
- » Age: 26
- » Home club: NSW Sapphires

Heather Garriock
- » Jersey #7
- » Age: 24
- » Home club: NSW Sapphires

Thea Slatyer
- » Jersey #13
- » Age: 24
- » Home club: NSW Sapphires

Clare Polkinghorne
- » Jersey #19
- » Age: 18
- » Home club: Queensland Sting

MIDFIELDERS

Alicia Ferguson
- Jersey #3
- Age: 25
- Home club: Queensland Sting

Joanne Peters
- Jersey #10
- Age: 28
- Home club: Northern NSW Pride

Collette McCallum
- Jersey #14
- Age: 21
- Home club: Western Waves

Sally Shipard
- Jersey #15
- Age: 19
- Home club: Canberra Eclipse

Lauren Colthorpe
- Jersey #16
- Age: 21
- Home club: Northern NSW Pride

Danielle Small
- Jersey #17
- Age: 28
- Home club: NSW Sapphires

FORWARDS

Caitlin Munoz

» Jersey #8
» Age: 23
» Home club: Canberra Eclipse

Sarah Walsh

» Jersey #9
» Age: 24
» Home club: NSW Sapphires

Lisa De Vanna

» Jersey #11
» Age: 22
» Home club: Western Waves

Kate Gill

» Jersey #12
» Age: 22
» Home club: Northern NSW Pride

Joanne Burgess

» Jersey #20
» Age: 27
» Home club: NSW Sapphires

SPOTLIGHT

Elise Kellond-Knight

Elise Kellond-Knight made her international debut for the Matildas more than a year before she made her debut in the W-League. At the time, there was no W-League, but that doesn't make Elise's career any less impressive.

Just four years after her Matildas debut, Elise was loaned out internationally to clubs in Germany and Japan. Her ability to play in both the midfield and back line has made her a key player for clubs the world over. As well as regular stints in the W-League, she's played in leagues across the USA and Europe.

Elise's skills have won her accolades that include being named on the All-Star Team for the FIFA Women's World Cup, 2011 and 2015™, as well as the honour of having now played more than one hundred games for the Matildas.

The CommBank Junior and Young Matildas

The Junior Matildas are Australia's national women's Under-17 team. They've been around since 2007, when Australia joined the Asian Football Confederation. At the time, the Oceania Football Confederation – which we'd been a part of since 1978 – didn't hold a tournament for the age group. But the AFC did! So when Australia made the switch from Oceania to Asia a national women's U-17 team was born.

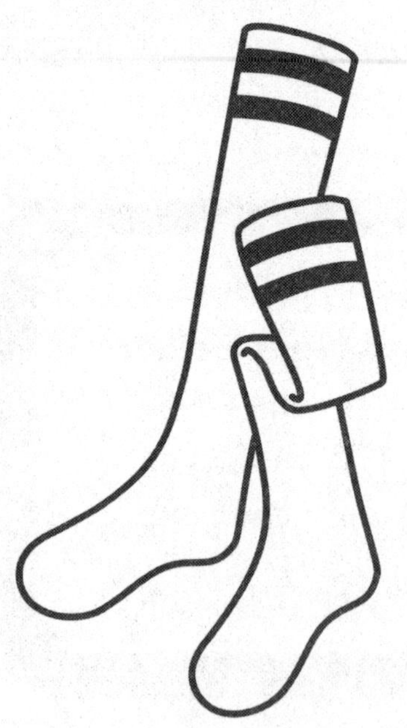

The Young Matildas have been around a little longer. They're Australia's national women's Under-20 team, and they were established when FIFA started holding the Under-19 Women's World Championship. (In 2006, FIFA raised the age limit of the championship to twenty.)

Just like the senior Matildas themselves, the Junior and Young Matildas compete in a number of international tournaments held by

FIFA, the AFC and the ASEAN Football Federation in their respective age groups.

Many of the current Matildas were members of the Junior or Young Matildas before joining the senior team, but not everyone.

There is one more women's national team competing at under-age level – the Under-23 Matildas. It's not a team that plays often, however, the AFF Women's Championship – for teams in Southeast Asia – is held for players over twenty, and in previous years the Young Matildas have competed in the biennial event. In 2022, the Australian U-23 AFF Championship squad included six players who had already played for the senior Matildas and fifteen players who had made appearances in the Young Matildas squad.

While the Junior, Young and Under-23 Matildas aren't senior international teams, that doesn't mean that the squad members don't play football in senior domestic leagues. That's particularly true for the Young Matildas. After all, players like Sam Kerr, Ellie Carpenter and Mary Fowler all made their

Matildas debuts at fifteen! Recent call-ups currently play for both state and national leagues in Australia as well as leagues in North America and Europe.

They also participate in training camps, with players from all over Australia coming together to work as a group, preparing for the rigours of international tournaments.

Regardless of whether they're in the Junior, Young or Under-23 Matildas squads, competing for a national team is invaluable experience for developing players, who benefit immensely from international tournaments, learning how to play against different styles of football and building competition experience.

It's also incredibly helpful for the staff of the senior team to observe and learn more about players in under-age squads. For coaches like Mel Andreatta (assistant coach of the Matildas), watching the next generation play on the international stage showcases the unique qualities of up-and-coming players and opens the possibilities of what the extended senior Matildas squad could one day look like.

When it comes to the next generation of Australia's national footballers, coaches have been spoilt for choice at every age level. More than sixty players are active at the Junior Matildas camps alone. In the last two years, more than seventeen players have made their senior debut for the Matildas. That's the same number of players that debuted across the six years from 2014–19! And the majority of them were once Junior or Young Matildas.

SPOTLIGHT

Kyah Simon

When Kyah Simon walked onto the field in her one-hundredth match for the Matildas at the 2020 Tokyo Olympics, she made history as the first Indigenous Australian player to reach the milestone. She's also the first Indigenous Australian to score at a FIFA World Cup, which she did just four years after her Matildas debut.

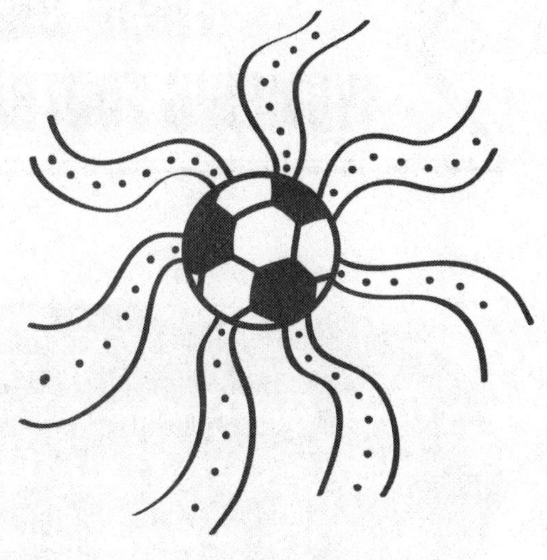

The beauty of football as a world game with plenty of common ground between players has given Kyah the confidence to stand up for her culture, showing support for Indigenous Australians on the world stage, like when the Matildas brought the Aboriginal flag onto the field of play in Tokyo. She uses her platform to inspire the next generation of First Nations footballers.

On the field, Kyah is known as a fierce attacker and top goal-scorer, as well as being a great sport who has been honoured as Player of the Match several times. They're skills that have seen her play for leagues in Australia, the USA, the Netherlands and, most recently, England's Women's Super League.

The Matildas on . . .

THEIR DREAMS FOR WOMEN'S FOOTBALL IN AUSTRALIA

That **girls** are given the exact **same opportunities as boys** in terms of development pathways.

Steph Catley

That people become **aware** of **how good** we really are.

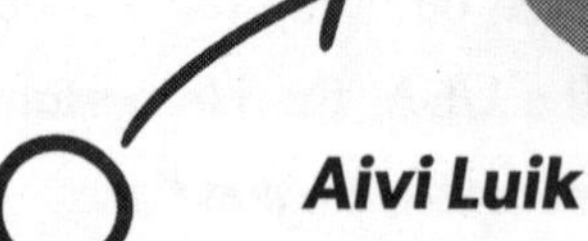

Aivi Luik

Hopefully be one of the **top one or two** ranked nations **in the world.**

Sam Kerr

To host the **World Cup** in 2023.

Ellie Carpenter

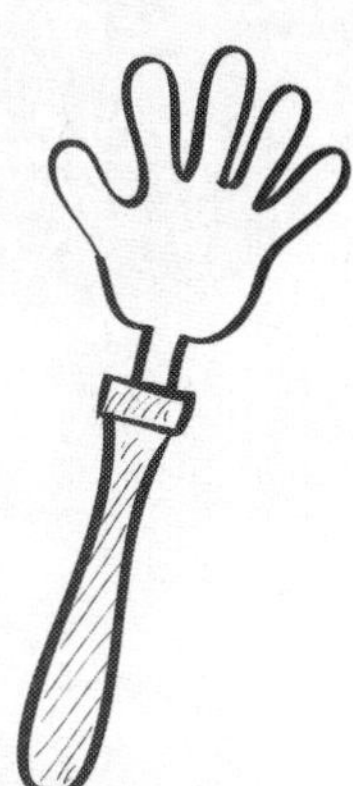

To **inspire** young girls and boys around Australia to **chase their dreams.**

Alanna Kennedy

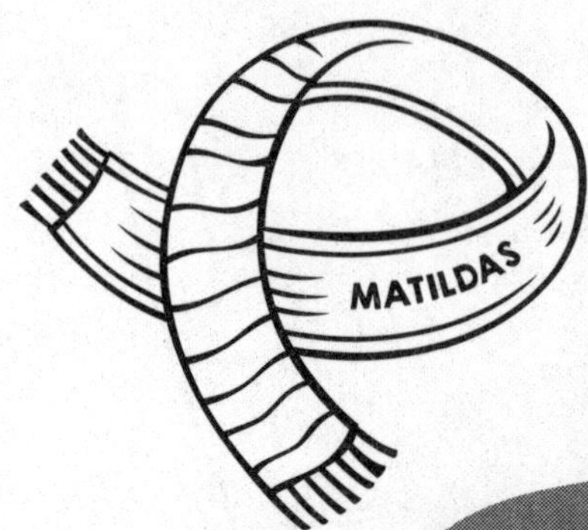

For all the Australian public to make **the Matildas** their **favourite sporting team.**

Laura Brock

To **engage** the fans, engage the public and really just **demonstrate how good we are** as a footballing nation.

Emily Gielnik

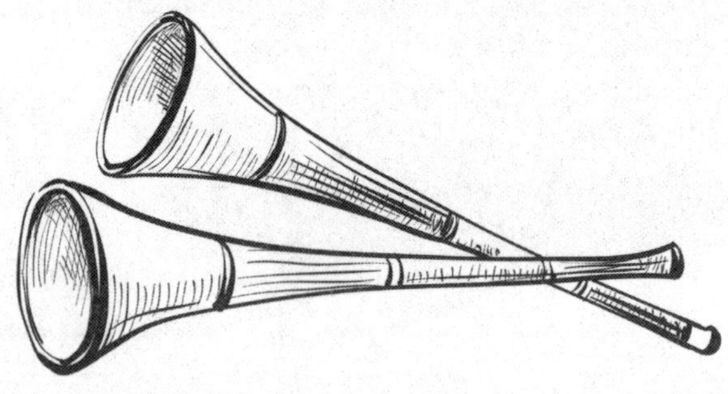

To leave a **lasting impression** of how Australians are.

Lydia Williams

To **continue this journey** for the future Matildas and the **next generation** coming through.

Emily van Egmond

THE IMPORTANCE OF CONSISTENCY

Talent and luck can play a big part in becoming a professional footballer, but something every Matilda knows is that a huge part of any athlete's success is training and consistency.

Even though the Matildas only play together a few times each year, they train constantly with their club teams to become the best players they can be. They often go above and beyond, too, adding their own training on top of what they do with their team.

Alanna Kennedy is amazing at free kicks – a skill she developed by practising *after* training almost every day until she was world-class. And Lydia Williams' amazing number of clean-sheet matches comes from training hard on her saves until she almost never lets a ball in.

Playing football at the elite level, the Matildas know that it's important to never stop practising the basic skills. Dribbling and passing might not seem like the most glamorous of skills for an international footballer, but consistent practice means that the team can consistently perform – and it helps them make sure any potential weaknesses are identified and rectified well before a match!

Being consistent also means sticking to the training schedule, even when the weather is bad or players are tired or motivation is low. Thankfully, consistency also means players train their bodies to know what they're supposed to do, so even if the player has to start a training session on autopilot, they soon get into the swing of things.

Consistency is especially important when players are coming back from breaks or injury. A slow, steady recovery to return to match fitness through rehab and a gently increasing training load requires consistent effort as well as the discipline not to jump ahead in the schedule and risk further injury.

It's not just training and injury rehab where consistency is important, either. One of the most important things about being a Matildas player is having the ability to perform at the elite level reliably and repeatedly. Consistency of quality play is what gets a footballer selected for the national team.

The 2011 World Cup campaign

The Matildas went into their FIFA Women's World Cup 2011™ campaign with a brand new benchmark after their previous results: runners-up in the AFC Women's Asian Cup and quarter-finalists in the 2007 World Cup. Could they do even better this time around?

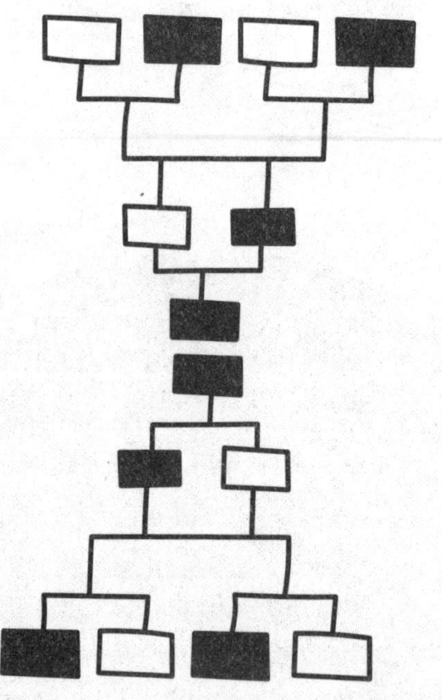

The 2010 Asian Cup was held in China, with eight teams battling to qualify for the FIFA Women's World Cup 2011™. Australia won their first two group matches, finishing 2–0 to Vietnam and 3–1 to South Korea. They lost their third match to China PR 0–1, but it didn't matter – the Matildas had placed high enough in their group to head into the semi-final knockout.

Winning the semi-final meant securing one of the coveted three automatic qualifying spots for the

FIFA Women's World Cup 2011™. The Matildas went into their semi-final against Japan eager to finish the match on top.

The problem was that Japan had finished the group stage with the best result out of all the teams: fourteen goals scored and only one conceded.

Both teams had everything to play for, and Japan put up a good fight, dominating possession in the first half. Then, in extra time at the end of the half, Kate Gill pushed through the Japanese defence and scored. Japan attacked aggressively in the second half, but the Matildas' defence prevented Japan from equalising and the match ended 1–0. The Matildas were not only going to be in another Asian Cup final, they were once again headed to the World Cup!

But first, they had one more Asian Cup game to play – the decider for Asian Cup Champion, against Korea DPR. The teams kicked off in misty rain and high humidity. Korea, the defending champion, attacked quickly, but couldn't stop the teenage Sam Kerr from scoring in just the nineteenth minute. The Matildas worked their defence as the rain got harder, but an equalising goal in the second half meant the game proceeded to a penalty shootout to decide the winner of the tournament.

Then, during the shootout, Australia scored five goals to Korea's four thanks to Kyah Simon converting the fifth and final penalty kick.

The Matildas had done it - they were the 2010 champions of the Asian Cup! It was also the first major AFC win of any Australian team - male or female - since joining the confederation years before.

A year later, the Australian team arrived in Germany, ready to meet the world's top teams at the World Cup. Sixteen nations were again competing for the top spot. Australia faced Brazil, Equatorial Guinea and Norway in their group stage, losing 0–1 to Brazil then winning 3–2 against Equatorial Guinea.

The Matildas' match against Norway was the decider for who would progress to the next stage. It was a tight game, with neither team making headway until the second half, when Norway scored the first goal in the fifty-sixth minute. Australia surged forward in retaliation and Kyah Simon equalised just one minute later. A second goal by Simon in the eighty-seventh minute secured the match for the Matildas – they were once again headed to the World Cup knockouts!

Australia's quarter-final match was against Sweden, then the world's fifth-ranked women's football team. Sweden scored two goals within the first sixteen minutes, setting the tone for the match that followed. Ellyse Perry scored for Australia in the fortieth minute, but Australia were ultimately unable to equalise and the game ended 1–3 after Sweden scored a third goal in the second half.

The Matildas finished their FIFA Women's World Cup 2011™ campaign having matched their 2007 performance, and ranked eighth in the tournament. Caitlin Foord was honoured with the Best Young Player award, and Elise Kellond-Knight was named as a defender on the All-Star Team of the Tournament. Lisa De Vanna and Kyah Simon were named as Player of the Match for two of the team's games. The Matildas had also raised their all-time World Cup ranking from fifteen in the FIFA Women's World Cup 2007™ to ten, cementing themselves as a team to be reckoned with!

The FIFA Women's World Cup 2011™ squad

GOALKEEPERS

Melissa Barbieri – co-captain
- » Jersey #1
- » Age: 31
- » Home club: Melbourne Victory

Lydia Williams
- » Jersey #18
- » Age: 23
- » Home club: Canberra United

Casey Dumont
- » Jersey #21
- » Age: 19
- » Home club: Brisbane Roar

DEFENDERS

Teigen Allen
- » Jersey #2
- » Age: 17
- » Home club: Sydney FC

Kim Carroll
- » Jersey #3
- » Age: 23
- » Home club: Brisbane Roar

Laura Alleway (now Laura Brock)
- » Jersey #5
- » Age: 21
- » Home club: Brisbane Roar

Ellyse Perry
- » Jersey #6
- » Age: 20
- » Home club: Canberra United

Elise Kellond-Knight
- » Jersey #8
- » Age: 20
- » Home club: Brisbane Roar

Servet Uzunlar
- » Jersey #10
- » Age: 22
- » Home club: Sydney FC

MIDFIELDERS

Clare Polkinghorne
» Jersey #4
» Age: 22
» Home club: Brisbane Roar

Heather Garriock
» Jersey #7
» Age: 28
» Home club: LdB FC Malmö (SWE)

Emily van Egmond
» Jersey #12
» Age: 17
» Home club: Canberra United

Tameka Butt (now Tameka Yallop)
» Jersey #13
» Age: 20
» Home club: Brisbane Roar

Collette McCallum – co-captain
» Jersey #14
» Age: 25
» Home club: Perth Glory

Sally Shipard
» Jersey #15
» Age: 23
» Home club: Canberra United

Lauren Colthorpe
» Jersey #16
» Age: 25
» Home club: Brisbane Roar

FORWARDS

Caitlin Foord

- » Jersey #9
- » Age: 16
- » Home club: Sydney FC

Lisa De Vanna

- » Jersey #11
- » Age: 26
- » Home club: Boca Raton magicJack (USA)

Kyah Simon

- » Jersey #17
- » Age: 20
- » Home club: Sydney FC

Leena Khamis

- » Jersey #19
- » Age: 25
- » Home club: Sydney FC

Sam Kerr

- » Jersey #20
- » Age: 17
- » Home club: Perth Glory

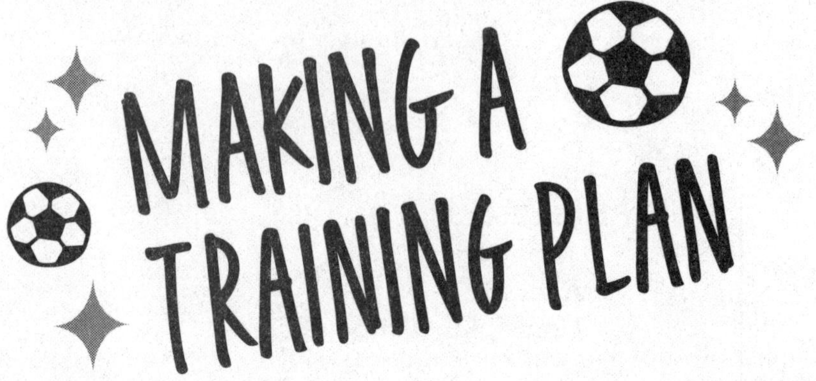

Matildas live and breathe football from a young age, going above and beyond their club training schedules to work on their skills, fitness and ball sense constantly. Here are some things to think about if you want to do the same.

A training plan can be a helpful tool to get started. You might want to approach this by picking some areas you know are weak points for you – for example accuracy of your passes – and focusing on drills that help improve them. Or you might want to cover a broad range of areas across a week. Most drills will help lots of different areas of your game even as you focus on one specific skill, but you can focus in on specific exercises. Perhaps you want to do accuracy-focused exercises on a Monday, then work on agility and reaction times on a Wednesday.

You could take a structured approach and block out time during the week where you'll spend time working on your ball skills, or your fitness, or you could say that your training plan is to have *no* training plan, and just spend every moment you can working on your football skills. You could even play with a ball between your feet while you're sitting down and watching TV!

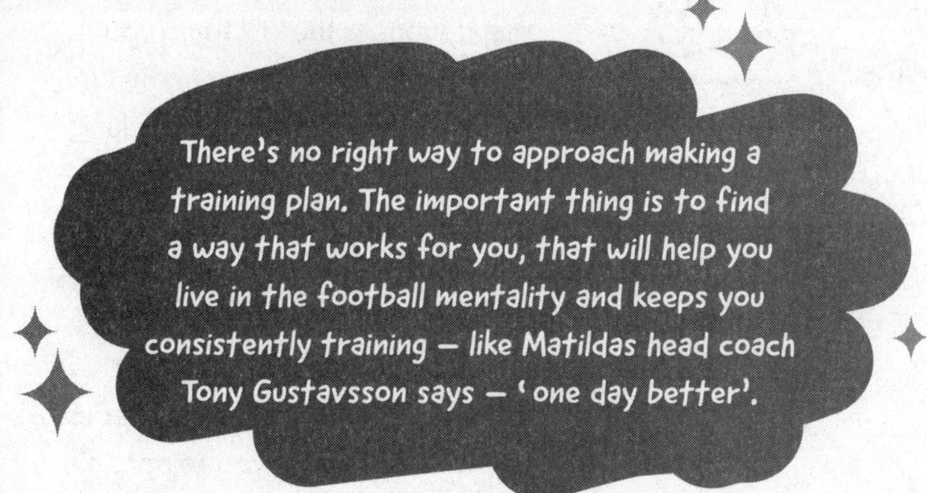

There's no right way to approach making a training plan. The important thing is to find a way that works for you, that will help you live in the football mentality and keeps you consistently training – like Matildas head coach Tony Gustavsson says – 'one day better'.

Maybe you'll decide to get up a bit earlier each morning and juggle in the backyard, or perhaps you're able to spend time some afternoons at the local park running drills between poles or against walls. Don't forget that even the Matildas incorporate repetition of basic skills into every training session, and that the simple exercise of kicking a ball against a wall helped them improve their first touch and stay match-ready during lockdown!

The examples of drills and variations throughout this book are just a few ways you can take a basic exercise and turn it into a whole training program of drills. And if you'd like a little help getting started, or taking your personal training to the next level, don't forget your coach is probably happy to give advice.

One of the most important things to keep in mind is consistency – training regularly and often. It's important not to burn yourself out to the point that training is the last thing you want to do! Keep your training fun by picking an activity – like kicking the ball against a wall, or juggling the ball – and make up unusual rules and challenges for yourself. Training doesn't need to be complicated.

If you have time you want to dedicate to your training but you're not able to spend it using a ball, think about things like improving your general fitness. Ball skills are important, but so is your ability to be quick when needed, as is having the endurance to last a whole match and train multiple times a week.

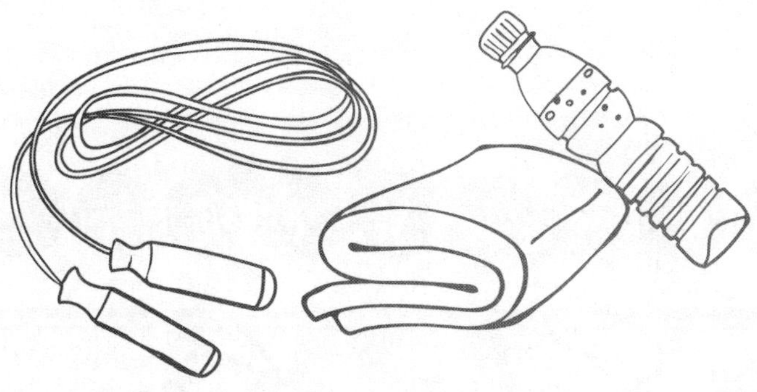

Skipping, for example, is an exercise you can do when you don't have much outdoor space to work with, and there are lots of ways to vary the activity to focus in on quick foot movements and coordination while working on your cardio fitness. Try exercises that work on your speed and agility too, like running as fast as you can between two points and turning abruptly each time you change direction.

And don't forget that being a successful footballer is as much about time spent off the ball as it is with a ball at your feet. Ensuring you give yourself time to rest and recover is super important – a lot of aspiring professional footballers are let down by injuries before their careers can take off. This goes double for mental health – take care not to burn out!

SPOTLIGHT

Sam Kerr

Sam Kerr is one of Australia's most successful and high-profile footballers – an incredible feat for someone who didn't start playing until she was twelve! Sam comes from a sporty family, and initially followed in the footsteps of her father and older brother, who have both played AFL professionally. When Sam was young there wasn't any capacity for women to pursue an AFL career, so Sam switched to football. Three years later, she made her Matildas debut.

Now, she's Australia's highest goal scorer (she overtook Tim Cahill's record in January 2022); has played football professionally for teams in Australia, the USA and England; and is the only female footballer ever to have won the Golden Boot in three leagues and across three continents.

In 2019, Sam was named captain of the Matildas – a huge honour that made her quite emotional. She's ushered the Matildas through several successful matches since then. She's also made over one hundred appearances for Australia.

Sam has played in the Women's Super League since 2020, when she made the move to England to play for Chelsea FC. She's helped the team win multiple trophies since then and has won the league's Golden Boot twice!

Sam's skills have been recognised outside of the footballing world too.

She's been honoured with both the Young Australian of the Year award and an Order of Australia Medal to recognise her achievements in the sport. She's also the first woman ever to appear on the global cover for EA Sports' FIFA game.

I CAN'T
Explain
HOW
PROUD
I AM TO BE A
part of this
TEAM
SAM · KERR

ALL ABOUT THE FANS

Over the lifetime of the Matildas, the national team has gone from a squad of women training in spite of the people throwing insults at them over the fence, to a hero-status team supported by millions of Australians at every turn.

Active Matildas supporters are groups of fans that have created chants and contribute hugely to the atmosphere of a game, singing nonstop around the stadiums. At every Matildas home game – and lots of games overseas – there's a screaming contingent of fans cheering the team on with the same 'Never Say Die' attitude that the Matildas have themselves.

Matildas fans have chants for the team as a whole and for individual players, cheering on players like Hayley Raso as she runs up the wing. The loud, intense support of fans gives back to the Matildas, buoying their spirits during the heartbreaking moments of a game and celebrating their wins when they happen.

This kind of support means the world to the Matildas, and it helps them lift their performance in matches even more than they already do. It's easy to become an active fan at a game. The chants are easy for anyone in the stadium to pick up. Or celebrating when things go the team's way can help the Matildas just as much. And remember to never stop cheering the team on – even when they're down. Active support can give the Matildas the boost they need to harness the 'Never Say Die' energy and come back from behind in games.

The Matildas have all kinds of fans – from the supporters who turn up to every match, to the people who watch the games at home. From past Matildas players and officials, to parents, to community participants and aspiring footballers. From grandparents to young kids and every age in between!

Fans love that the Matildas are great role models for people of all ages. The team's drive, passion, strength, authenticity and willingness to better themselves is inspiring to fans young and old. And the work that the Matildas do off the pitch is just as important to see as the work they do on it. The Matildas often give their time to fans with photos, autographs or a quick conversation.

Plus, they provide something for girls to aspire to – after all, some of the fans in the crowd might be Matildas one day themselves.

Stories and Advice from the ParaMatildas

What's your favourite drill?

Probably the Tic Tac Toe relay. It's fast, it's fun and the girls get really into it! It becomes quite competitive.

- Georgia Beikoff

What's the most valuable piece of advice you received on your path to being a ParaMatilda?

That we are undefeated. That no matter what is happening, to never ever give up, because 'undefeated' wasn't about winning, it was about believing in yourself and in your team.

- Tahlia Blanshard

SPOTLIGHT

Alanna Kennedy

DOB
21 January 1995

14

2021/22
MANCHESTER CITY (ENG)

Campbelltown, New South Wales

Defender

SENIOR DEBUT

Sydney FC
2010

MATILDAS DEBUT

Australia vs New Zealand
friendly match
June 2012, aged 17

Football wasn't Alanna Kennedy's only sporting love as a kid – she was a Little Athletics champion, holding several records in hurdles, long jump and high jump, and competing in the New South Wales cross-country championships. Eventually, she had to make the choice between athletics and football. Obviously, football won!

Alanna usually plays defence, but she's also a capable midfielder. She's also known for her free kicks – a skill she's practised to make it world class. Like many other Matildas, Alanna didn't have a lot of access to female footballers as role models growing up. Now that she's an adult, she prioritises connecting with the next generation – particularly girls – and helping them see what can be achieved in the world of sport. She's an ambassador for Cadbury's Women in Sport program and Macarthur FC – the A-League team based in her home town.

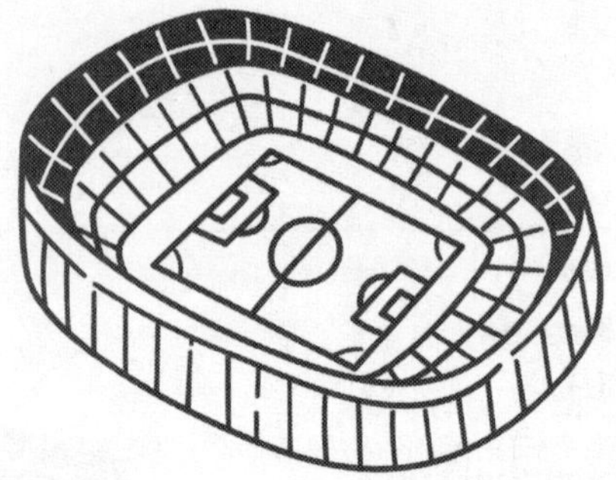

Alanna's represented Australia at every major tournament the Matildas have competed in since 2012, and a lot of other matches too. She's played more than one hundred international games, including the Olympic qualifier against Brazil that she captained in her home town, and number one hundred itself, another match against Brazil that she again captained.

Off the field, Alanna's easy-going attitude has served her well. She never stops trying to improve herself as a player and a person, and always tries to find something positive to focus on in every experience.

She wants to be remembered for the kind of person she is, and for doing her part to make the game of football better.

I THINK THAT'S HOW YOU
WIN
THINGS
BY DOING IT

TOGETHER
and for
Each Other
ALANNA KENNEDY

The 2015 World Cup campaign

By the time the 2014 AFC Women's Asian Cup rolled around, the Matildas were Australia's most successful football team *ever.* They went into the 2014 tournament as reigning champions, arriving in Vietnam in May keen to defend their title.

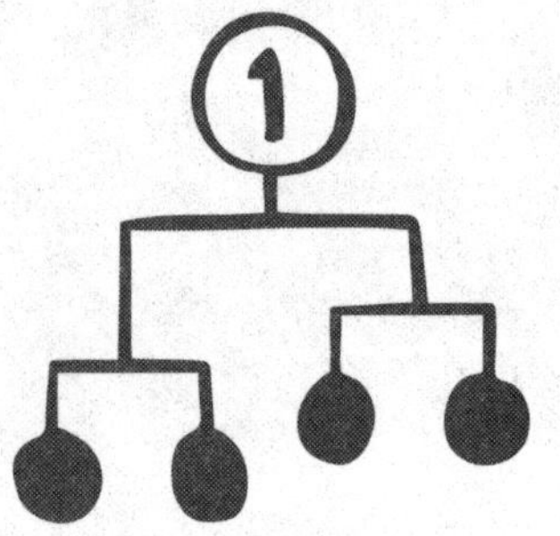

For the first time, five teams from Asia would qualify to progress to the FIFA Women's World Cup 2015™. This was because FIFA had increased the number of qualifying finalists from sixteen to twenty-four thanks to the growing popularity of the women's game across more countries, and more slots were available to the different football confederations. As long as the Matildas passed the group stage they were guaranteed a spot.

The Matildas drew their first Asian Cup group match against Japan. Goals by Caitlin Foord and Lisa De Vanna had Australia in front until close to the end of the game, when an unfortunate own goal was followed by a goal by Japan.

The next two group games went better, with the Matildas securing 3–1 and 2–0 wins against Jordan and Vietnam. Australia qualified second in the group, moving on to both the semi-final knockout stage and the World Cup!

The Matildas faced South Korea in the semi-final. Hot and humid conditions saw the score remain nil-all until the second half, when Australia scored two goals to South Korea's one, sending the Matildas into the final. Facing Japan for the second time in the tournament, the Matildas were unable to match their earlier performance and the game finished 0–1. Australia had to settle for runners-up for the 2014 Asian Cup.

The Matildas headed to Canada in 2015 along with twenty-three other nations in the fight for the World Cup. They played the two-time world champions – the United States – Nigeria and Sweden in their group stage, losing, winning and drawing the respective matches to secure themselves second spot in the group and progress to the knockout stage. It was a fantastic result, particularly against Sweden, who had eliminated Australia from the World Cup four years earlier.

With twenty-four teams now competing in the World Cup, the 2015 knockout stage included a round of 16 before progressing to quarter-finals. Australia faced Brazil in a close match that saw neither team able to make headway until the eightieth minute, when Kyah Simon scored a goal off a rebound. Brazil was unable to equalise, and the Matildas were through to a World Cup quarter-final again. That wasn't the only thing worth celebrating though.

For the first time in the country's football history, an Australian team (women's *or* men's) had won a knockout game in a World Cup!

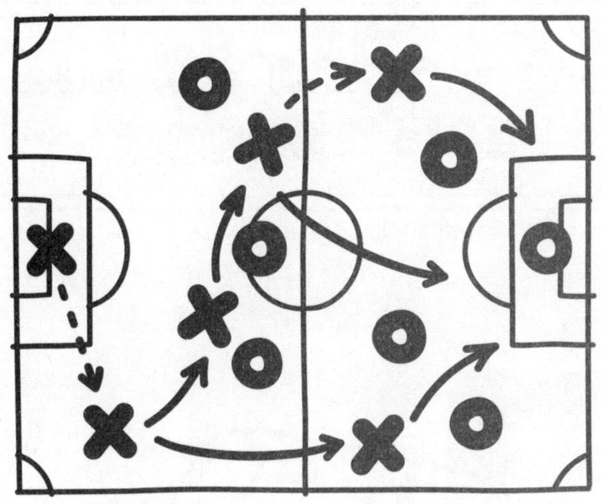

The Matildas had a battle ahead of them in the quarter-final. They were facing Japan, the reigning World Cup champions, who hadn't yet lost a match during the 2015 tournament. Australia played well, successfully defending against Japan during the first half but also unable to convert any chances of their own. Goalkeeper Lydia Williams saved multiple shots, but a goal in the eighty-seventh minute put Japan in the lead. Unable to equalise, Australia's World Cup campaign came to an end.

Nevertheless, the Matildas had showed just how much their game had improved. Both Elise Kellond-Knight and Lisa De Vanna were named on the All-Star Team of the Tournament – the second appearance for each player. Both women were also commended as Player of the Match for their performance in the group stage, with Kellond-Knight receiving the award for her performance during the knockout round of 16. Australia exited the tournament positioned as seventh, having been able to seriously challenge some of the world's top five teams and were later ranked by FIFA as ninth in the world.

The FIFA Women's World Cup 2015™ squad

GOALKEEPERS

Lydia Williams

- » Jersey #1
- » Age: 27
- » Home club: Canberra United

Melissa Barbieri

- » Jersey #18
- » Age: 35
- » Home club: Adelaide United

Mackenzie Arnold

- » Jersey #21
- » Age: 21
- » Home club: Perth Glory

DEFENDERS

Clare Polkinghorne

» Jersey #4
» Age: 26
» Home club: Brisbane Roar

Laura Alleway (now Laura Brock)

» Jersey #5
» Age: 25
» Home club: Brisbane Roar

Servet Uzunlar

» Jersey #6
» Age: 26
» Home club: Sydney FC

Steph Catley

» Jersey #7
» Age: 21
» Home club: Melbourne Victory

Elise Kellond-Knight

» Jersey #8
» Age: 24
» Home club: Brisbane Roar

Alanna Kennedy

» Jersey #14
» Age: 20
» Home club: Perth Glory

MIDFIELDERS

Emily van Egmond

» Jersey #10
» Age: 21
» Home club: Newcastle United Jets

Tameka Butt (now Tameka Yallop)

» Jersey #13
» Age: 23
» Home club: Brisbane Roar

Katrina Gorry

» Jersey #19
» Age: 22
» Home club: Brisbane Roar

Nicola Bolger

» Jersey #22
» Age: 22
» Home club: Sydney FC

FORWARDS

Larissa Crummer
- » Jersey #2
- » Age: 19
- » Home club: Brisbane Roar

Ashleigh Sykes
- » Jersey #3
- » Age: 23
- » Home club: Canberra United

Caitlin Foord
- » Jersey #9
- » Age: 20
- » Home club: Perth Glory

Lisa De Vanna – captain
- » Jersey #11
- » Age: 30
- » Home club: Melbourne Victory

Leena Khamis
- » Jersey #12
- » Age: 28
- » Home club: Sydney FC

Kyah Simon
- » Jersey #17
- » Age: 23
- » Home club: Sydney FC

Sam Kerr
- » Jersey #20
- » Age: 21
- » Home club: Perth Glory

Michelle Heyman
- » Jersey #23
- » Age: 26
- » Home club: Canberra United

SPOTLIGHT

Tameka Yallop

At fourteen, Tameka Yallop (nee Butt) was already playing for an all-age (senior) women's football team – she was just that good. Then her tactical skills caught the attention of the selectors for the Queensland Academy of Sport's women's squad. Soon, she was debuting for the Junior Matildas, then for the Brisbane Roar in the inaugural W-League season, then the senior Matildas – a possibility she hadn't even known existed until a couple of years earlier!

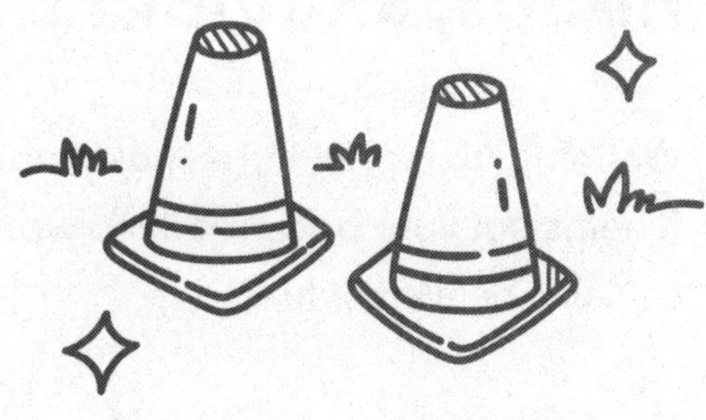

Tameka plays as an attacking midfielder, a key part of the Matildas' success. She's represented Australia in countless tournaments and more than one hundred matches – including the Tokyo Olympics, where she scored in the very first match. Her skills have also earned her spots in club teams across Canada, the USA, Germany, Japan, Sweden (where she met her now-wife!) and England. And at home, she was the first ever Brisbane Roar player to score fifty goals for the club.

Heads, Shoulders, Knees and Cones!

Warming up is one of the most important parts of any training session. It helps get your body ready to work, gets your head in the game and can also be a lot of fun!

The Matildas have developed some unique drills to help them warm-up for an epic training session. You've probably danced along to the song *Heads, Shoulders, Knees and Toes* before. Well, the Matildas have turned the concept into a warm-up game they call Heads, Shoulders, Knees and Cones.

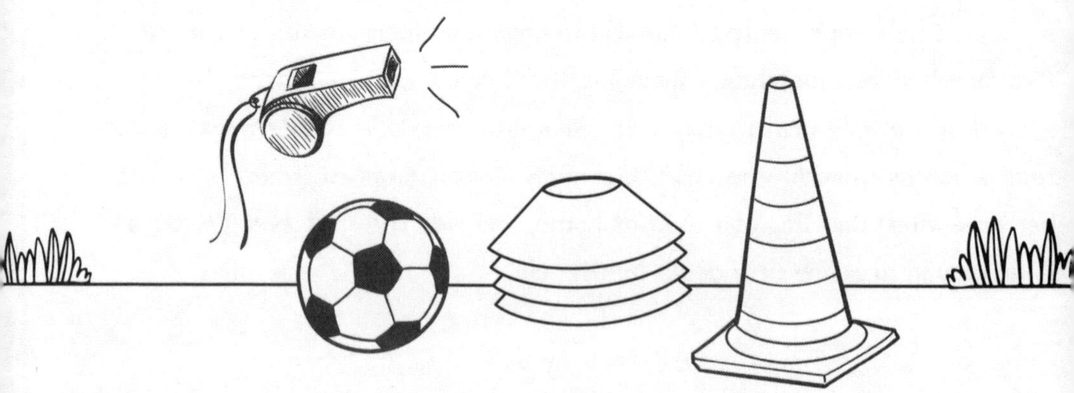

To do the drill, split your team into pairs of players and give each pair one or more cones to place on the ground between them. The key thing to remember is that if you're using two or more cones per pair, each cone should be visually distinct.

There are lots of different ways you can do this! The Matildas use different coloured cones, but you could also make your groups of cones unique by . . .

Writing numbers on them

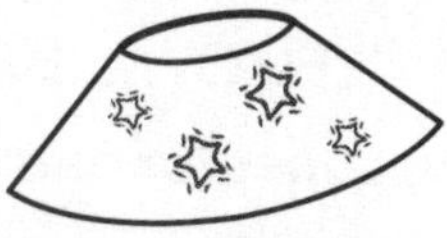

Using stickers to decorate them

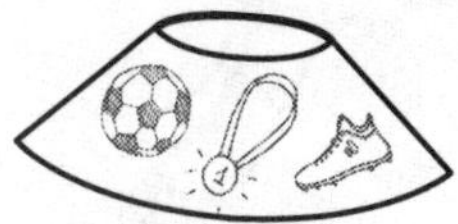

Drawing different designs on them

The important thing is that each player in the pair can clearly see which cone is which, and that every pair receives the same set of cones as everyone else.

HEADS

SHOULDERS

CONE

DOTS

YELLOW

Once each pair of players has their set of cones, your coach will start calling out the words 'heads', 'shoulders', 'knees' or the words that describe your sets of cones! Players have to touch the body part called out with both hands, and be ready to grab down to the ground and pick up the right cone before the other person in their pair!

If, like the Matildas, you're using different coloured cones, this could sound like: 'knees', 'shoulders', 'knees', 'knees', 'YELLOW'. If your team only has enough cones for one cone per pair, you could hear: 'heads', 'knees', 'shoulders', 'knees', 'CONE'. Or if you've separated your groups of cones using, say, polka dots and triangles that you've drawn on the cones, you might hear: 'shoulders', 'heads', 'shoulders', 'DOTS'. Your drill is limited only by your imagination.

There are plenty of ways to make this drill harder as your team starts to warm up. The Matildas start the drill by kneeling on the ground, just warming up their bodies from the knees up.

For the next stage of the drill, they stand up, adopting a wide leg stance that allows them to react quickly to grab the cones from the ground!

For the final stage of the drill, they add the extra challenge of jogging on the spot with quick, light foot movements to ensure their bodies are well and truly ready to start training in earnest.

Player Pathways

The Matildas are the pinnacle of women's football in Australia, but how does a future Matilda become part of the team?

It's important to remember that the pathway to a professional career isn't linear. A player doesn't need to go from A, to B, to C in a straight line, where missing a step on the way means your dreams of becoming a Matilda are over. Instead, the pathway to being a professional footballer involves layers of skills and experiences gained by playing in different leagues at different levels, with support programs like the Skill Acquisition Program (SAP) or academies that help players improve even more.

How do you get those layers? Well, the pathways for girls to play in senior leagues begins at the

community club level. Most likely you already do this! Playing for your local club is the perfect way to build your skills and prime yourself for the next step in your football journey. After all, playing in their local club comp is where most Matildas started out!

It's probably not news to you that most club teams are filled with players from the same geographical area – usually a suburb or district. Each club team plays in a local football league against teams from other clubs in the area. But did you know that most leagues have their own talent development teams (though structures differ from city to city and across states)?

For example, Quakers Hill Junior Soccer Club (where Kyah Simon started playing) competes in the Blacktown District Soccer Football Association (BDSFA) development leagues competition, fielding teams across multiple age groups and divisions five – two. The club also fields division one teams, which compete in a BDFSA league called the performance league.

Above the club level, the BDSFA has Under-14, 15 & 17 semi-professional teams – called the Blacktown Spartans (who Courtney Nevin played for). The Spartans compete in the National Premier League (NPL), which is the highest league at district and state level. They also run regional talented player development programs to help girls make the leap into a semi-professional team. Most district football associations will do the same.

If your league doesn't have development or performance teams or programs, you can apply to join one nearby. It's a great way to get noticed by people looking for talented players to progress to higher levels. Scouts for state teams that compete in national talent identification championships and centres like State Academies or Institutes of Sports will often come along to see who might progress to be a Matilda one day.

Another way to build your skills and experience – and make sure that scouts hear about your footballing prowess – is to attend a sports high school, like Ellie Carpenter and Alanna Kennedy did. These are selective schools that specialise in helping students develop skills in their sport.

Scouts also attend matches at the highest club (division one) and district (NPL) levels, as well as training camps and other development programs. Sometimes your team might get a heads up that a scout will be attending a match, or sometimes you won't find out until afterwards. Either way, if a scout watching your match likes the way you play, you might be invited to play at an even higher level, or train with some of the best coaches in the country.

Scouts and coaches could also be looking for players to join the Junior and Young Matildas. Playing for a junior state side is one of the best ways to be noticed by the Matildas coaches at different levels!

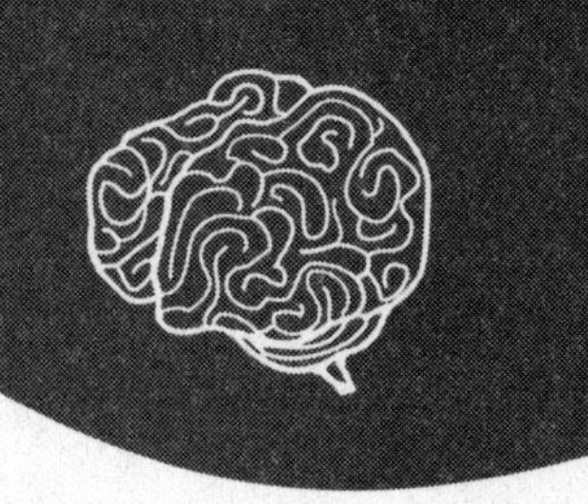

It's important to look after your life off the field too – take care of your diet, mental health and make sure you rest enough so you don't burn out before your footballing career has even begun.

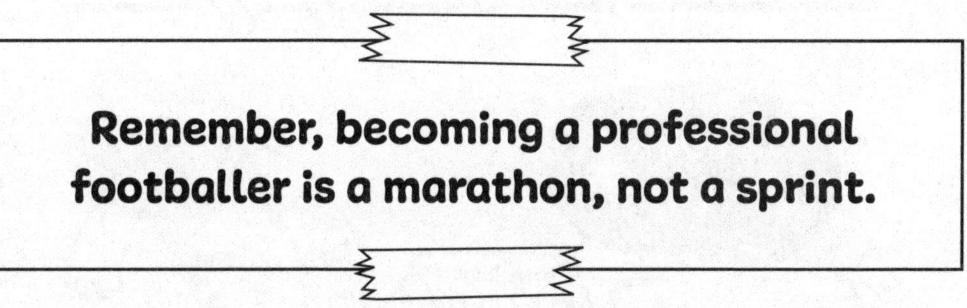

Remember, becoming a professional footballer is a marathon, not a sprint.

And if you're at the beginning of your football journey and already feeling behind, don't forget that you don't have to be a proven star early on or even have been playing football your entire life to become a Matilda. Sam Kerr didn't start playing until she was twelve!

SPOTLIGHT

Steph Catley

DOB
26 January 1994

SENIOR DEBUT

Melbourne Victory
October 2009

MATILDAS DEBUT

Australia vs New Zealand
friendly match
June 2012, aged 18

Steph Catley started playing football when she was six, after begging her mum to let her play in the boys' team – she was the only girl on the roster! Now there's a girls' team in that same local comp named the Catleys in her honour. Steph made her senior football debut playing for Melbourne Victory in 2009 and has been a firm favourite in Australian women's football ever since!

Steph is left-footed and began playing football as left winger. She's kept the number seven (typically reserved for attackers) ever since – even though she now plays left back for the Matildas! She's played more than one hundred games for Australia, including the Rio 2016 and Tokyo 2020 Olympics.

She's recognised as one of the best footballers in the world, but it's not just her skills on the field that stand out – it's who Steph is as a person that her friends and family are most proud of. They say she's a fantastic leader, humble and always there for the people she cares about.

The fight to be taken seriously

Despite the Matildas' performance in tournaments, when they successfully became the first Australian football team to survive a World Cup knockout match, in 2015 they were receiving contract payments beneath the minimum wage. This meant players were holding down second or even third jobs to make ends meet while trying to find time to train and compete.

So, just before they were due to head off on a tour of the United States in September 2015, the Matildas went on strike. They were outperforming the Socceroos in big tournaments, but the women's game still wasn't receiving the same treatment as the men's. They had less funding, limited access to adequate training facilities and far, far less recognition and media attention than the Socceroos.

Much like the pioneering female footballers in Australia, the Matildas were still making enormous sacrifices to play for their country. Without access to the same level of facilities and coaches that the men's team had, the Matildas were unable to truly reach their potential when they faced the world's best teams.

It wasn't just better pay and working opportunities that the Matildas wanted. They also wanted to secure better development opportunities for the next generation, ensuring that there were pathways for girls across Australia to play football, all the way from childhood club competitions to professional careers. They wanted to protect and help build the future of Australian women's football.

It took two months of strike action, supported by their players' union – and missing the US tour – but the Matildas finally received better salaries and a commitment to better investment and better resources in the women's game. Four years later, women's football in Australia scored another win with an agreement with Football Australia, the national body, that brought the Matildas' working conditions up to the same level as those enjoyed by the Socceroos.

Because of the efforts of the 2015 Matildas, women in Australia can now dedicate their careers to playing football and realise their full potential in the world game.

The Matildas had massive successes without the same facilities, salaries or treatment that the men's national team enjoyed, and now they finally have the opportunity to play on an even field.

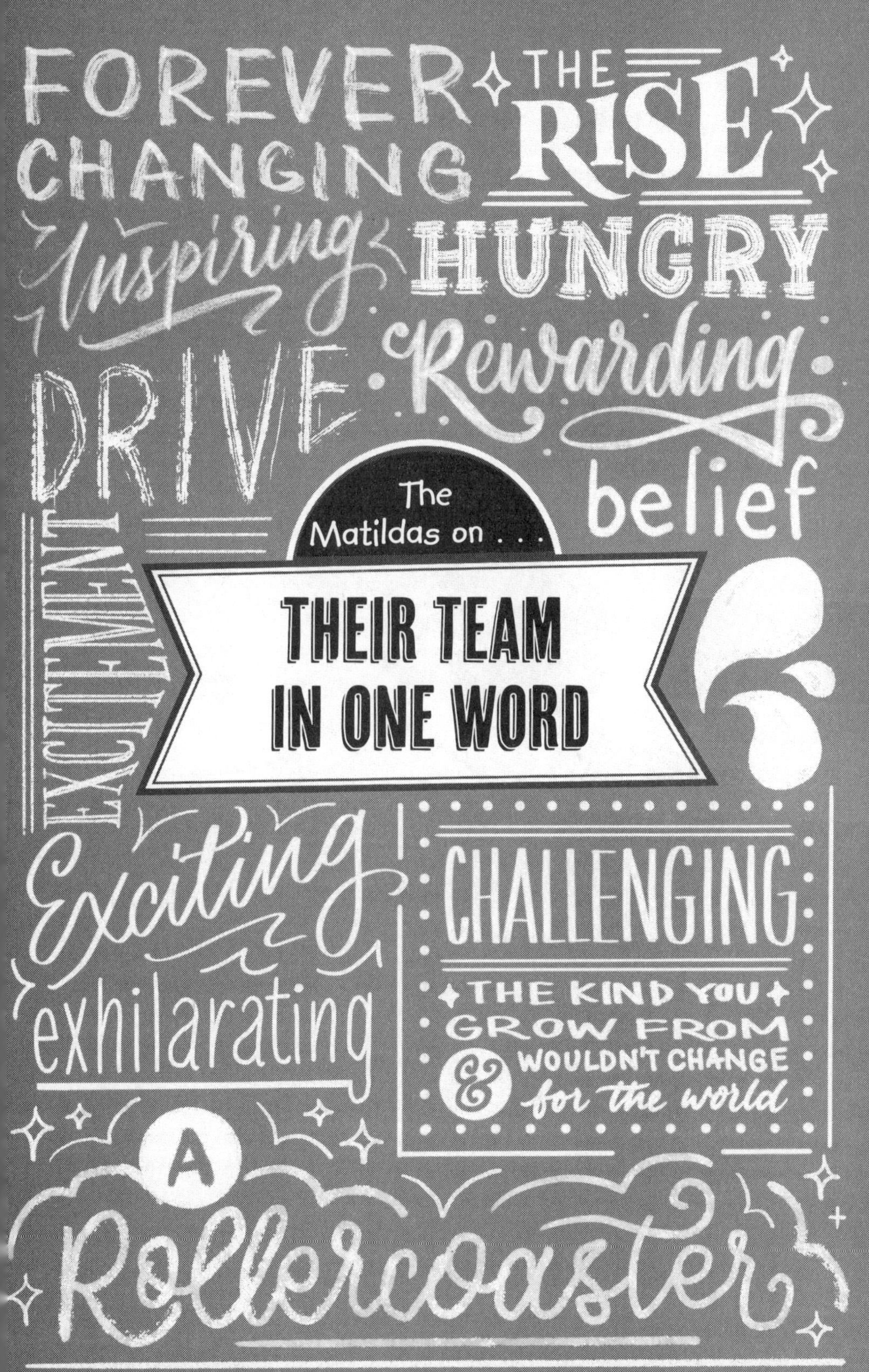

FOREVER CHANGING
THE RISE
Inspiring
HUNGRY
DRIVE
Rewarding
belief
EXCITEMENT
The Matildas on . . .
THEIR TEAM IN ONE WORD
Exciting
exhilarating
CHALLENGING
THE KIND YOU GROW FROM & WOULDN'T CHANGE for the world
A Rollercoaster

SPOTLIGHT

Caitlin Foord

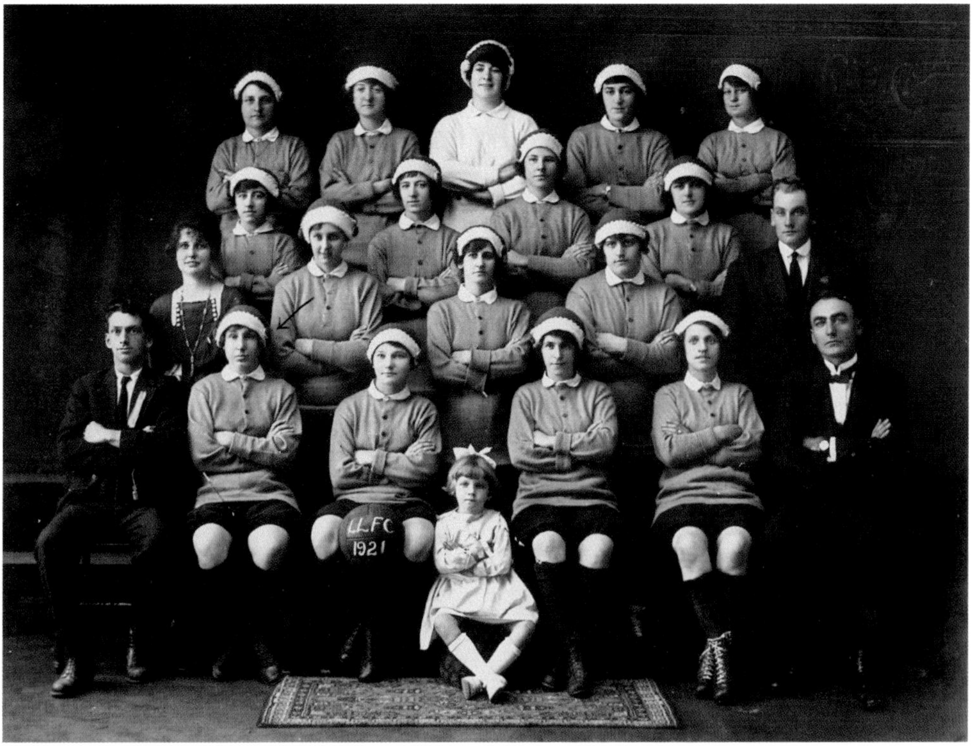

LATROBE LADIES' FOOTBALL CLUB.

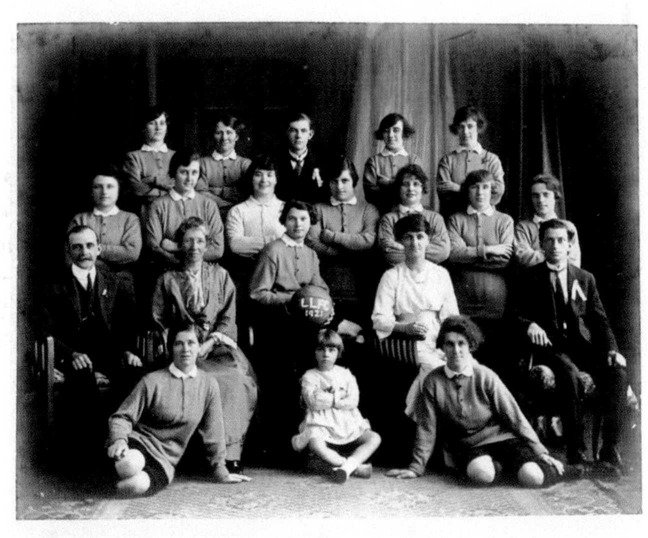

BACK ROW.—L. Bryen, M. J. McDonnell, W. Martin (Vice Pres.), J. Bryen, I. Bryen.
STANDING.—L. Yates, G. Gehrman, G. Wenlock (Vice Capt.), E. Yarrold, P. Summers, T. Robinson, E. Powell (Treas.)
SITTING.—F. Power, Mrs. Tate (President), E. Ide (Captain), Mrs. J. T. Gilday (Patron), R. J. Powell (Organiser).
FRONT.—B. Fowler, Mavis Powell, M. Hannah.

Mum 2nd on Right 2nd Row

One of Australia's first female football teams – the Latrobe Ladies, from Brisbane, Queensland.

Before the hosts of the FIFA Women's World Cup 2023™ were announced, the Sydney Opera House was lit up by images of Australian women and girls playing soccer.

The moment it was announced that the Australia-New Zealand bid had won!

The ParaMatildas squad, coaches and officials at the inaugural IFCPF Women's World Cup.

Lainee Harrison in action.

The ParaMatildas' very first starting five, from left to right: Georgia Beikoff, Lainee Harrison, Tahlia Blanshard, Katelyn Smith (GK) and Eloise Northam (C).

Georgia Beikoff and Eloise Northam celebrate a goal.

To keep their skills fresh outside of tournaments, the Matildas often play friendlies against other national teams. Here, they line up before a 2021 friendly against Brazil . . . and celebrate their win after the game has ended.

The moments before – and celebrations after – Mary Fowler scored a goal against Brazil.

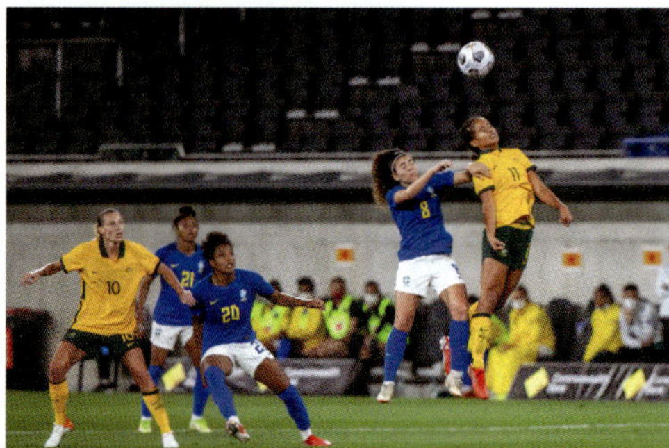

The Matildas in action against Brazil.
From top: Ellie Carpenter attacks, the team anticipates the incoming ball, Mary Fowler and Emily van Egmond on form, returning to the game after a team huddle.

From top: head coach Tony Gustavsson gives advice during the half; Alanna Kennedy heads the ball; Caitlin Foord, Kyah Simon and Alanna Kennedy during a quiet moment; Caitlin Foord and Steph Catley talk to a referee.

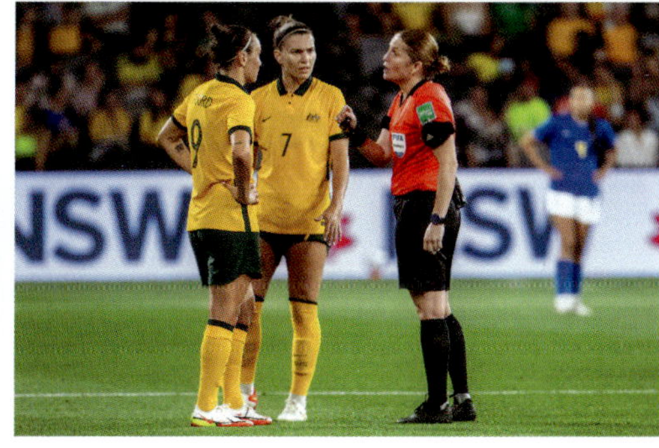

No matter where the Matildas play, their fans are always there to support them!

The Matildas know how important a proper warm-up is to playing their best game.

McDonald Jones Stadium in Newcastle lights up before a friendly match between the Matildas and the USA.

Starting players and subs alike gather for one last team huddle before the game begins!

Goalkeepers Lydia Williams and Mackenzie Arnold are integral to the team's success.

Lydia Williams in action.

The Wiggles are big fans of the Matildas too! They performed a pre-match concert before Australia faced the USA for a friendly match in Sydney.

The Matildas in action versus the USA in Sydney.

From top: Caitlin Foord, Emily van Egmond goes for a header, Steph Catley on the ball, Tameka Yallop races to intercept.

Sam Kerr shares some last thoughts with the team before they face the 2020 Tokyo Olympic gold-medal-winning Canadian team in a friendly match.

The Matildas in action!
Clockwise from top left: Sam Kerr, Emily van Egmond, Clare Polkinghorne and Alanna Kennedy.

Caitlin Foord had only just started her senior football career for Sydney FC when she made her Matildas debut. She was impressive from the very start, scoring a goal in her first match for Australia!

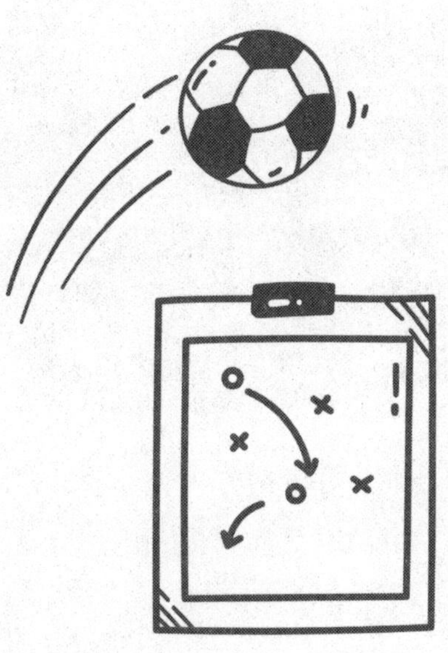

Caitlin plays as a forward now, but it hasn't always been that way. When she played for the Matildas at the FIFA Women's World Cup 2011™, she played almost all of her matches as a defender. Her ability (and willingness) to adapt makes her a great footballer – she's never afraid to change her role for the good of the team, or to assist other goal scorers when needed.

On the pitch, she's fantastic at anticipating where the ball will land and converting her chances into goals – a skill she's worked hard to develop. The Matildas – and Arsenal, her home team – score more consistently when she's in the game thanks to the opportunities she creates. In training, Caitlin works hard to constantly adjust her technique, always seeking to be that little bit better.

Caitlin's dedication to her craft has impressed her coaches worldwide. She's played professionally for teams in Australia, the USA, Japan and England in her career. She's won multiple football awards, and was also given the honour of captaining her one hundredth match for Australia – a friendly against the New Zealand Football Ferns in 2022.

Professional Football
Around the Globe

When the Matildas play for Australia, it's only a small part of their sporting calendar. For most of the year, they play for clubs in national league competitions like the Liberty A-League in Australia.

But it's not just clubs in the Liberty A-League that members of the team call home – the Matildas are in demand across England, Europe and the USA. Of the twenty-three women who formed the 2022 AFC Asian Cup squad, seventeen play for clubs outside Australia.

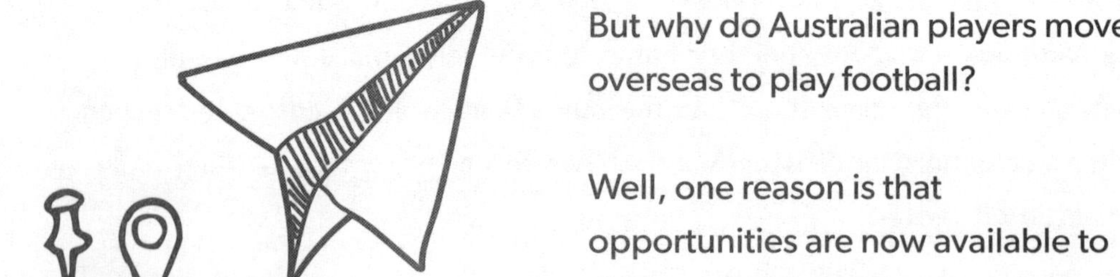

But why do Australian players move overseas to play football?

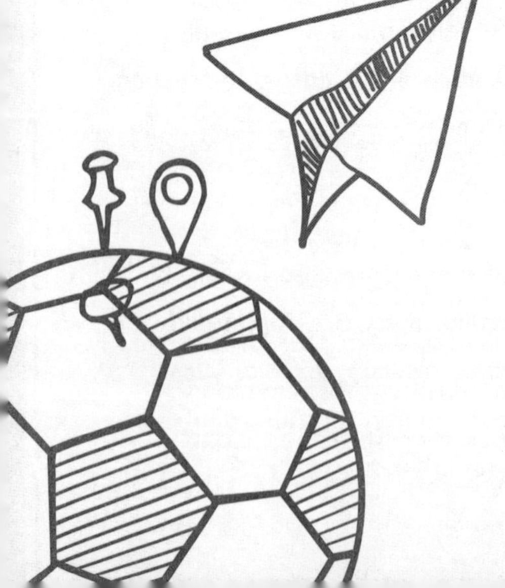

Well, one reason is that opportunities are now available to them with big professional clubs in burgeoning leagues, and another is to learn different styles of football. The way the game is played in Australia is different to the way it's played in the USA, which is different

again to the way it's played in England, which is different *again* to the way it's played in France and so on and so forth.

By playing in different leagues and being exposed to different styles, the players are able to play with a high level of international players, and learn new skills, or new ways to execute existing skills, that help them continually improve and push themselves forward.

Another reason is to maximise their time playing professional football. The regular season of the Liberty A-League runs for three months, whereas England's Women's Super League runs across eight months and offers players almost twice as many games. For European teams, there's the potential for even more games if they make it to the UEFA Women's Champions League.

This schedule allows players to have a proper, long season and then a break, ensuring they are able to systematically work on their skills and fitness with different coaches without overtaxing their bodies.

With Matildas players competing in more than half-a-dozen different leagues worldwide, coming back together to train as a team does have some challenges. Firstly, professional club commitments can overshadow national team activities, but FIFA sets specific 'windows' during the year when clubs have to release their players for national team commitments. Also, many of the leagues finish at different times, so individual players will sometimes arrive at training camps at different times to others. And because of various team commitments, the squad will sometimes only get a handful of friendly games together to regain their rhythm before they need to perform in a competitive match.

Players take it all in their stride as professional footballers because the benefits are well worth it. Tony Gustavsson, the current head coach, expects that Matilda-level players spend time at clubs that allow them to reach their full potential and take their time playing professional football to the max. And for many of the Matildas, they believe overseas clubs give them that best opportunity for now. And it's not just themselves and the national team that our internationally based footballers are helping.

The increase in Australian women playing in international leagues is opening more and more doors for the next generation. At the FIFA Women's World Cup 2019™, seven of the top eight teams in the quarter finals were from Europe. The other team was the now four-time world champions USA. The Matildas' assistant coach, Mel Andreatta, thinks the domination of European teams is thanks to the setup of their football environments, which are geared to help players flourish.

Our players have benefitted massively from the increased levels of professional support, becoming better footballers themselves and helping their teammates do the same. Together, they're pushing the ceiling for Australia's professional female footballers higher than ever.

Stories and Advice from the ParaMatildas

What's your favourite junior footballing memory?

My favourite junior footballing memory was when I used to rush to my home computer after school to watch Ronaldinho do his insane football tricks on YouTube, then I'd go into the backyard and practise them myself until I mastered them!

- Nicole Christodoulou

How do you handle pre-match nerves, especially when you're facing a scary team?

I have breathing exercises that help me keep focused - not worry about how they play but to only focus on our game. When we begin to play how the opposing team wants us to play, that's when things get hard. I find when we breathe, it helps us to stick to our game plan.

- Georgia Beikoff

SPOTLIGHT

Lydia Williams

When Lydia Williams was a kid, her parents moved to Canberra and signed her up to play football to help her make friends. The top team had all the players it needed, bar one: Lydia could play Division One if only she was willing to be the goalie. The rest is history!

Lydia is a Noongar woman – the daughter of a Noongar man and American mum. Seeing Cathy Freeman proudly holding the Australian and Aboriginal flags at the 2000 Olympics inspired her to become an elite athlete. Now, she's a role model herself.

Lydia made her Matildas debut when she was seventeen. It was a bittersweet moment without her dad, who passed away just before he could see her represent Australia on the international stage. He always knew she could do it though.

Now, Lydia has played more than one hundred games for Australia (the first female goalkeeper to have done so) in multiple World Cups and two Olympics. She is the longest-serving Matilda ever, has played for clubs in Australia, the USA, England and now in France, has been recognised with multiple football awards and has been inducted in to the Aboriginal and Torres Strait Islander Sports Hall of Fame.

WOMEN SUPPORTING WOMEN

Being a Matilda isn't just about playing football – it's also about being part of an international community of women who show up for important causes off the field too.

For example, in 2022, Aivi Luik's brother was diagnosed with brain cancer. To honour him, she organised a fundraiser for a very important cause: brain tumour research: If the footballing community could help her raise $30,000, she would shave her head.

Donations poured in, and Aivi reached her goal after only four days! That same night, the Matildas were facing New Zealand's Football Ferns. On the opposing team was Rebekah Stott, a defender who's played for New Zealand since 2012 and also played for Melbourne City in the Liberty A-League.

In 2021, Rebekah was diagnosed with Hodgkin's lymphoma – a cancer that affects the lymphatic system. She had to take almost an entire year off from football while she underwent treatment including chemotherapy. The Matildas versus Football Ferns match was one of her first international games back on the field.

When the full-time whistle blew, the teams gathered together and Rebekah shaved Aivi's head. It didn't matter that Aivi and Rebekah were on different national teams. The footballing community rallied together to support Aivi supporting her brother. It showed just how much female footballers are in it together – supporting each other through the hard times even when they're on opposing teams.

The camaraderie between the Australian and New Zealand teams, that started in 1979 with the very first A-international game in Sydney, was also the perfect metaphor for the #AsOne bid that won Australia and New Zealand the right to co-host the FIFA Women's World Cup 2023™.

Even though the Football Ferns are the Matildas' oldest rivals, the relationship between both countries continues to be strong and supportive.

SPOTLIGHT

Katrina Gorry

Like many of the senior Matildas, Katrina has competed in multiple tournaments for Australia – including the 2016 Olympics, where she appeared in all four matches.

Unlike many of the current senior Matildas though, she didn't play the 2020 Olympics, but it was for a pretty special reason: she was pregnant.

Since the birth of her daughter, Katrina has made a huge effort to return to the world of elite football. She worked closely with physiotherapists to manage her training load and was soon back on the field playing for Brisbane Roar. She's a skilled midfielder with more than a dozen international goals under her belt – not to mention those she's sunk for her club teams. Katrina plays in the Swedish Damallsvenskan league, and has also been loaned back to Brisbane Roar. She's already been selected into the Matildas squad for 2022.

The Matildas at the Olympics

Football has been an Olympic sport for men since 1900, but it wasn't until 1996 that women's football was included in the Games.

Much like qualifying for the World Cup, teams qualify to compete in the Olympic Games based on their performance in previous tournaments. For the 1996 and 2000 Olympics, teams qualified based on the results of the previous year's FIFA Women's World Cup quarter-finals. Since the 2004 Games though, qualification has been done in a similar way to how teams are selected for the World Cup: each confederation has held a tournament to decide who will represent them.

Because they finished twelfth in the FIFA Women's World Cup 1996™, the Matildas didn't qualify for the first appearance of women's football at the Olympic Games. They didn't rank high enough in 2000 either, but it didn't matter – the Summer Olympics were held in Sydney that year, and as the host country, Australia got an automatic entry along with the top seven teams from the previous World Cup. The Matildas were going to be able to represent Australia on home soil at the biggest multi-sport event in the world! Participation in the Olympic Games marked a significant turning point in the popularity, progress and funding of the women's game.

2000 Sydney Olympics

The Matildas trained hard – not just at football, but also to prepare themselves for the sheer scale of an Olympic tournament. At the beginning of their training sessions they'd walk out and sing the national anthem, then play while their coach blasted noise to simulate the sound of 35,000 screaming fans. It still couldn't prepare them for the moment they walked into the Games' opening ceremony – remembering the absolute roar of support that greeted them still gives the players goosebumps.

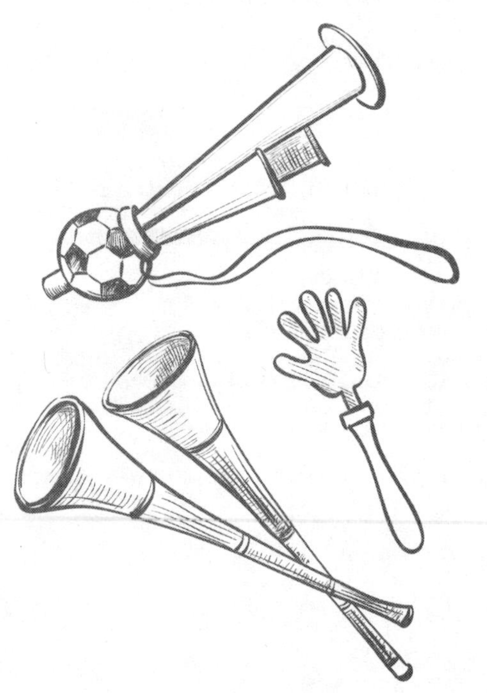

During the Games, Australia faced Germany, Sweden and Brazil. They lost the first match (which was the very first event of the 2000 Olympics!) and the last, but drew against Sweden. It wasn't enough to see them through to the knockout stage, but they'd proved they could compete at an intensely high level of football, finishing seventh overall. Over 85,000 people had showed up to watch the three games – a record attendance for women's football in Australia that stood for almost two decades.

2004 Athens Olympics

In 2004, each confederation held their own qualifying tournament. Australia was still a part of the Oceania Football Confederation at this point, competing against Papua New Guinea and Fiji for the chance to be one of ten teams in an expanded Olympic program. The Matildas qualified top of the table and arrived at the Athens Olympics ready to show the world how far they'd come.

In the group stage, the Matildas lost to Brazil, won against Greece and drew with the United States, finishing third on the table and securing themselves a quarter-final spot. In the quarter-final, Sweden scored two goals in the first half and Australia went into the break 0–2. A goal by Lisa De Vanna in the seventy-ninth minute gave the Matildas hope, but they were ultimately unable to equalise and were out of the competition. Regardless, it was a fantastic tournament for Australia – the Matildas had improved on their previous Olympic performance, not only making it out of the group stage but finishing fifth in the overall rankings.

When Australia entered the Asian Football Confederation in 2006 and competition for Olympic spots became much fiercer – there were ten teams ranked in the FIFA top fifty at the time, compared to just one in the Oceanic Football Confederation.

Qualifying for Olympic spots was made even more difficult in 2008, because the Games would be hosted by China, who automatically took one of the two available spots for Asia in a twelve-team competition. Two Olympic Games came and went before the Matildas qualified again. They finally had success at the 2016 qualifiers – the team was off to Rio!

2016 Rio Olympics

The number of women's teams in the 2016 Olympic Games had increased from ten to twelve teams.

The Matildas' campaign had a rocky start, with the team conceding the fastest-scored goal in Olympic history to Canada in the very first minute of their first match.

The Australian team was unable to equalise and the game ended 0–2 after Canada scored a second goal in the eightieth minute.

The second group match, against Germany, was incredible, with the Matildas threatening a massive upset against the then world number two team. Sam Kerr scored in the sixth minute, and a goal by Caitlin Foord in the forty-fifth minute cemented Australia's turnaround. Germany fought back, equalising by the end of the match for a 2–2 draw.

Australia won their third match, against Zimbabwe, and finished the group stage with enough points to move through to the quarter-finals.

The knockout match against Brazil was a complete deadlock. The Matildas were almost perfectly matched by the Brazilian team, with each side alternating domination of the game for almost equal possession. Brazil had more technical football skills, but Australia was harder working and the game was intensely frenetic from the start. The final whistle blew on a 0–0 score, sending the match into a penalty shootout after 120 minutes of play.

The shootout was as nailbiting as the match itself, with both teams netting four goals before the fifth shooter for each team was thwarted. Another three players for each team stepped up, with Brazil scoring three goals to Australia's two. The game was over – 6–7 on penalties.

Australia left the 2016 Rio Olympics having once more made it to the quarter-finals, ranked seventh overall, having held their own amongst the world's best teams and extremely proud of their performance in the tournament, after giving it everything they had.

SPOTLIGHT

Hayley Raso

Every professional athlete has their share of injury stories – from small injuries that knock them out of a game, to bigger ones that mean the end of a season. Hayley Raso has a more intense story than most: in 2018 she got a knee in her back while playing a club game for Portland Thorns.

In a single moment, three vertebrae were fractured and she wasn't sure if she'd ever walk again, let alone play.

Incredibly, less than a year later, Hayley was walking . . . back out onto the field for Brisbane Roar! Then she played for Australia at the FIFA Women's World Cup 2019™, appearing in all four of the Matildas' matches. Now she's made the move to the Women's Super League in England, playing the 21–22 season for Manchester City, where her skills as a versatile player capable of playing up front or on the wing has already seen the team bring home trophies.

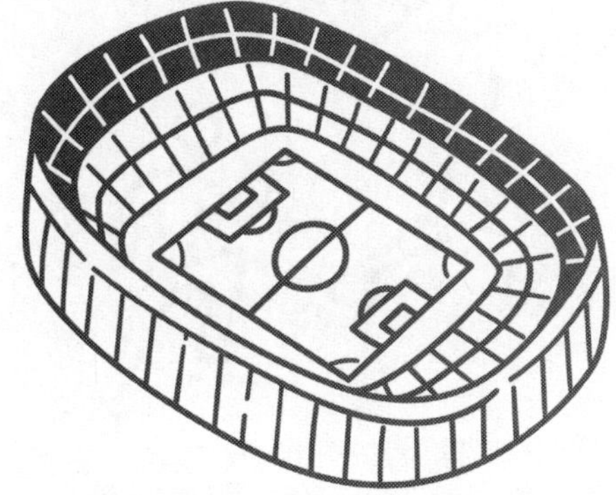

Inside a Matildas Training Camp

Playing for a national team isn't the same as playing for a club. Where club teams train together week-in, week-out, often playing games once or more each week during the football season, the Matildas are part of club sides *and* the national team – and they don't play for Australia anywhere near as regularly.

Take the Matildas squad that played the 2022 AFC Women's Asian Cup. Of the twenty-three footballers on the squad, six players compete in Australia's Liberty A-League, ten play in England's Women's Super League and the remaining seven play in various leagues around Europe and the USA. Between them, they play for sixteen different clubs!

This means that when it's time for the team to come together ahead of international games, they need to spend dedicated time learning to play together again. That's where training camps come in.

A couple of weeks before a tournament is due to start, the Matildas squad will come together for an intense training camp.

Sometimes the camps are held on home soil, but often the squad will meet somewhere close to where the tournament is being hosted. For the 2022 Asian Cup, which was held in India, the team's training camp was in the United Arab Emirates. This helps players have time to get over jet lag, get assessed by national team medical staff, ideally get used to the climate in which they'll be playing and avoid long haul flights occurring too close to competition matches.

Because the Matildas play for different clubs in different leagues all over the world, they have lots of different commitments on their time. Sometimes, it can take days for the entire squad to assemble in one place. Some players will have come from season breaks, and some will come from leagues where they've been playing nonstop.

The first days of camp are always about shaking out the legs and starting to work together as a team. The coaches will work with the players more individually as they wait for the entire squad to assemble, ensuring that no session is wasted.

Then, as the team comes together, the focus shifts. Coaches and players pay attention to the little details that can make or break a game, ensuring the team is ready to fire at one hundred per cent of their potential. It's also the time for the Matildas to practise their signature style – something that's important when playing styles can be completely different in different leagues!

Training camps cover a wide range of sessions. Players undergo medical assessments and physiotherapy, spend time dissecting videos of their performance in training and matches, do sessions in the gym and, of course, put in hours on the field. Warming up is one of the most important parts of physical training, so players spend a lot of time on prehab – jogging, stretching and working on their mobility to ensure they're reducing their risk of injury as much as possible.

Field sessions usually last sixty to one hundred and twenty minutes and can include lots of different types of training. The goalkeepers have their own dedicated coach, and often train separately to the team to hone their specialised skills. For the rest of the team, drills that focus on speed, agility, accuracy and teamwork are super important. The Matildas get on the ball quickly in their training sessions to maximise their time practising skills.

The field sessions focus a lot on repetition of the most basic skills, like one-touch passing – the basics can never be drilled too much!

They also spend time on tactical sessions and practising set pieces specifically geared for dealing with their upcoming opposition.

As important as training camps are for honing technical skills, they're also vital for ensuring the squad's teamwork is at its peak. For many of the Matildas, the only time they play together is when they're appearing for the national team, so time spent fostering their friendships and learning where each player shines is one of the most valuable outcomes of camp. That's especially important for the newer selections and players gearing up to make their debut, who might never have trained or played with some (or all) of their new teammates before.

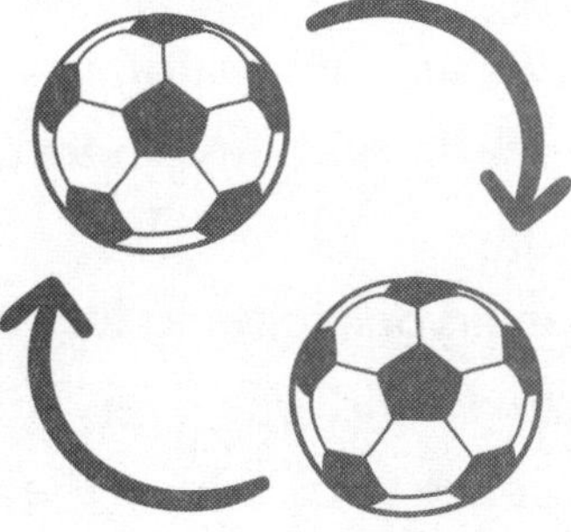

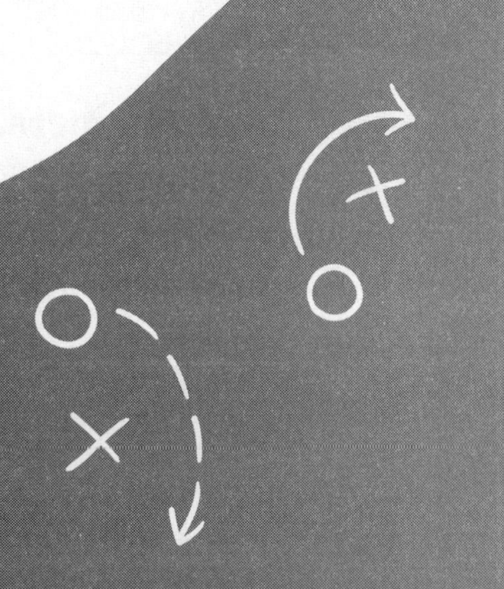

And while the camps allow players to focus on training without the distractions of everyday life, what happens outside of sessions is equally as important. The players get time to hang out, rest and recover and generally enjoy the atmosphere of immersing themselves in the excitement that comes with preparing for an international tournament or game. The downtime is just as important as the training!

The time out of training is also where younger players can turn to experienced Matildas for guidance. Veterans of the squad like Aivi Luik can offer a wealth of advice to the newer team members, mentoring them and acting as role models. In fact, head coach Tony Gustavsson actually encouraged Luik out of retirement to do exactly that for the 2022 Asian Cup, noting her character, professionalism and attitude to be just as important as her standout performance on the field.

With everyone looking forward to what's ahead, focusing on what they have to do and with everyone's excitement building, it's an amazing experience to be part of the national team. Cohesion and morale builds and players get more confident in themselves and their squad.

After immersing themselves in their preparations, the Matildas leave their training camps ready to take on the world's best teams at their upcoming tournaments!

SPOTLIGHT

Ellie Carpenter

Ellie Carpenter is only twenty-two, but with more than fifty appearances for the Matildas under her belt, you'd be forgiven for thinking she was older!

Ellie grew up on a farm hundreds of kilometres west of Sydney, and her early footballing days involved hours of driving just to get to matches and training – sometimes up to seven hours round trip.

At fifteen, Ellie signed with the Western Sydney Wanderers and became the youngest person in what was then called the W-League. Six months later, she made her full senior debut for the Matildas. When she signed with the Portland Thorns in 2018, she became the youngest player in the history of the United States' National Women's Soccer League. Ten days after her debut for the team, she became the league's youngest goal-scorer too.

After several seasons playing in Australia and the USA, Ellie made the move to Europe. She's been with the French team Olympique Lyonnais since 2020, quickly becoming an integral member of the team and helping them take out the Champions of France title in the Division I Féminine league and become UEFA Women's Champions League champions.

But in the 2022 Champions League final, Ellie ruptured her anterior cruciate ligament (ACL). It knocked her out of action for at least six months – which could include the FIFA Women's World Cup 2023™.

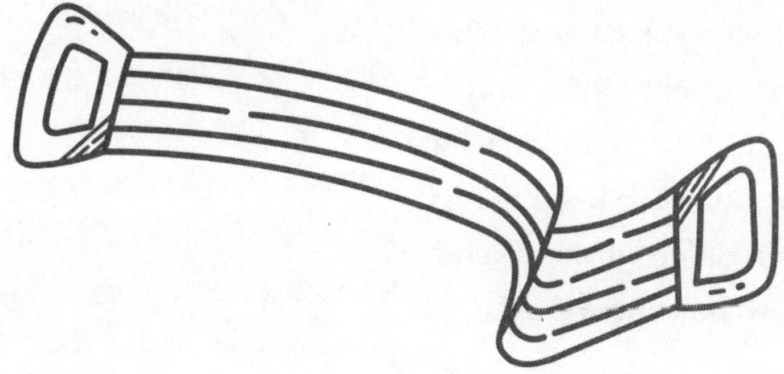

Drills with . . .

A BALL AND A WALL

One of the great things about football is that you can work on your skills almost anywhere. Being a Matilda isn't only about the training you do with your team. Elite footballers build their skills over years of playing around with a ball.

During the COVID-19 pandemic, a lot of the Matildas needed to train alone to maintain their skills and fitness levels while in lockdown. One of the best things they could do during this time was simply just kick a ball against a wall. The repetition is super helpful, and there are countless variations that can be introduced to keep things fun and train different skills – and all you need is a ball and a wall!

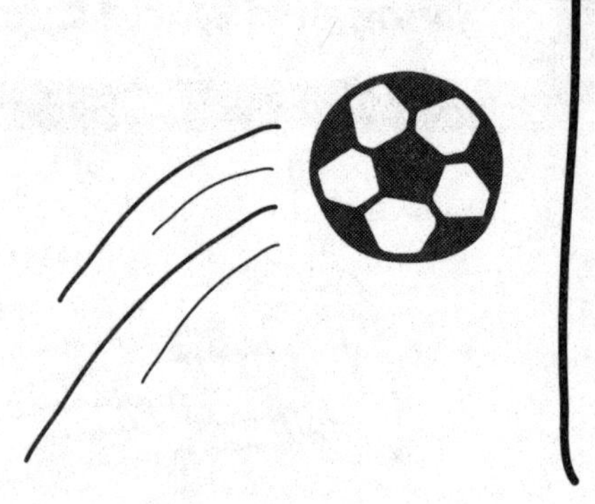

Having a backyard is great for this kind of training, but it's not essential. Your local park probably has a toilet block or another structure you could use.

One of the simplest exercises you can do is to kick the ball at the wall over and over again – practising both passing or shooting and trapping, using both feet – but there are *heaps* of ways to mix it up!

Setting yourself a target on the wall to aim for, then try and hit it each and every time. You could change this up again by moving closer or further away every few kicks.

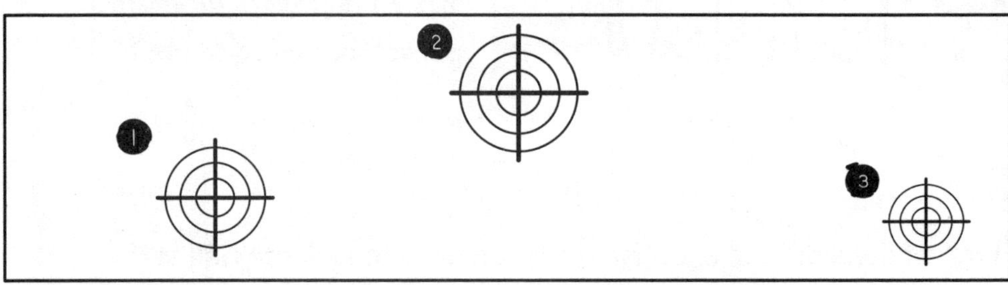

Set two or three targets and aim for each alternately. Maybe one is higher than the others, and one much further to the right. On kick one, you hit your original target, then the next kick, aim for the higher target, then on the third kick you aim out to the target on the right.

Train your reaction time by moving close to the wall – ideally less than a metre away. The idea is that the ball should be back at your feet almost as soon as it leaves them. Try challenging yourself to kick and control the ball with the same foot, and then do the same with the other foot. You'll have to be both quick and nimble if it rebounds in an unexpected direction!

You can also train your reaction time using the above method and both feet. You should be close enough to the wall that if you kick the ball with one foot and control it with the other, both feet need to be in the air at the same time. This trains your nimbleness and your ability to predict the ball's behaviour.

Make the exercise easier or harder by varying the power you put behind each kick.

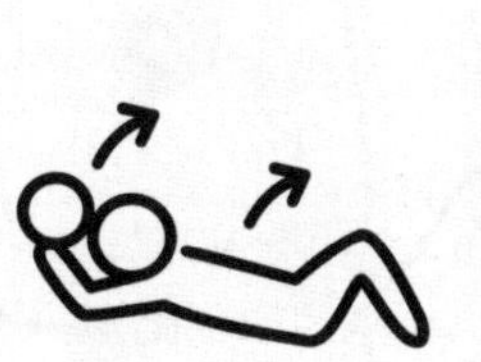

It's easy to create drills using a ball and a wall that *don't* involve kicking too. Combine throwing and catching the ball with doing stomach crunches – lie flat on the ground and hold the ball in both hands behind your head. In one movement, crunch up and throw the ball at the wall. You'll catch the rebound on your way down from the crunch before you're flat again. It's super useful for goalkeepers, but also improves hand-eye coordination and reaction times for footballers who play other positions as well. Plus it helps train your abdominal core.

The variations are limited only by your imagination!

SPOTLIGHT

Chloe Logarzo

Chloe Logarzo was already a seasoned international player by the time she made her debut for the Matildas in 2013 – just two months earlier, she'd captained the Young Matildas through to the finals of the AFF Women's Championship.

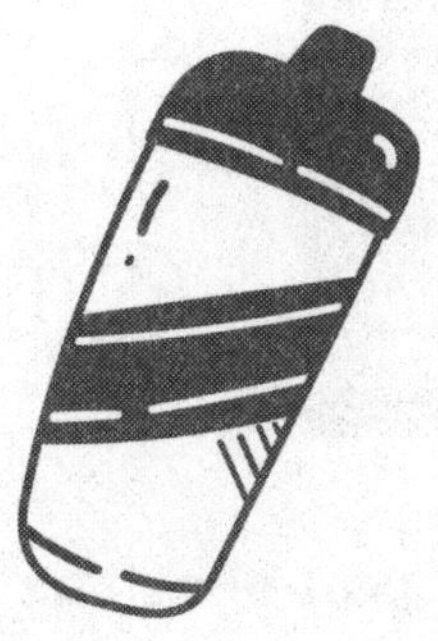

Chloe's now played more than fifty games for the Matildas in her career (including appearing at two Olympic Games), as well as playing domestic leagues the world over. She was the second Matilda to sign a contract with an English Women's Super League team in 2020, but then made the jump to Kansas City – one of the few Australian players to move to the USA from Europe!

In September 2021, she tore her ACL and has been undergoing the long road to recovery since then, really taking the time to build her pre-season fitness from the ground up. Luckily, Chloe is back in the Matildas squad in 2022 after rehabilitation and hard work.

The 2019 World Cup campaign

After Japan beat the Matildas in the 2014 AFC Women's Asian Cup final, and then knocked them out of the FIFA Women's World Cup 2015™, the Australian team headed to the 2018 Asian Cup in Jordan ready to prove how much they'd improved their game against the defending champions, Japan.

Before coming face to face with Japan though, the Matildas had to get through their first two group matches. Up first was South Korea. Both sides played strongly, but neither was able to score and the game ended in a draw. Next, Australia played Vietnam in a very different match, with the game ending 8–0 in the Matildas' favour. The third group match was against Japan!

The game was a nailbiter from the start, with the teams playing a close-fought contest that seemed destined to end in heartbreak for Australia when Japan scored in the sixty-third minute. The goal slid the Matildas down to the third spot on the table, their place in the Asian Cup semi-final and their chance at heading to the FIFA Women's World Cup™ seriously at risk. And then, with four minutes left, Sam Kerr scored an equaliser that catapulted Australia back to the top of the group. The game ended 1–1, with Australia onto the semis *and* the World Cup.

Much like their tournament so far, the Matildas' semi-final match against Thailand was nothing short of dramatic. Australia had beaten them 5–0 in a friendly just a month before, but this game wasn't as smooth sailing. Thailand played a spectacular game in the Asian Cup, sending the match into a penalty shootout when the whistle blew on a 2–2 draw after extra time. The Matildas scored three penalties to Thailand's one, thanks to Mackenzie Arnold's fantastic saves. A few hours later, Japan beat China PR in their semi.

So, just like in 2015, the Matildas were going to face Japan for the title once more.

Everything was on the line, and though Australia dominated from the start they were unable to convert their chances at goal – the Japanese keeper saved everything the Matildas could throw at her. The score was 0–0 at half-time, with the game open for the taking. In the eighty-fourth minute, Japan broke stalemate, and the Matildas were unable to equalise. With a final score of 0–1, Australia were runners-up again in the Asian Cup.

The FIFA Women's World Cup 2019™ was held in France. The Matildas squad was ready to face Italy, Brazil and Jamaica in their group, with a blend of young and experienced players – a true golden generation of Australian footballers.

The first match, against Italy, got off to a good start when Sam Kerr netted her first World Cup goal in the twenty-second minute with a converted penalty, and Australia went into half-time ahead. Italy equalised at fifty-six minutes and, with no more goals scored, the game went into injury time. Australia had multiple chances to score again, but ultimately it was Italy who scored and the game ended 1–2 to the Italians.

In match two, the Matildas were up against Brazil, keen to repeat their 2015 performance. Australia's chances didn't look promising just before the half – Brazil had scored two goals to Australia's zero, and it seemed the teams were going to head into the break with the Matildas firmly behind. Then, in extra time, Caitlin Foord scored! The Matildas came out fighting in the second half – the momentum of the game had changed and the stadium was full of excitement. Chloe Logarzo equalised in the fifty-eighth minute, and then an own goal by Brazil locked in the team's first group loss in a World Cup in twenty-four years. Australia won the match 3–2.

Australia's last group match, against Jamaica, was history in the making. Sam Kerr became the first Australian to score a hat-trick at a senior World Cup, and then incredibly scored a fourth goal that pushed Australia into second spot in the group and secured their win over Jamaica 4–1. The Matildas were through to the round of 16!

Australia faced Norway in their knockout match. Both teams were unable to convert opportunities and, even though Australia played well from the kick off, Norway soon pushed through the defence to score in the thirty-first minute. Australia couldn't equalise and went into the half-time break down 0–1. Things started looking up in the second half when Sam Kerr slotted the ball past the Norwegian keeper in the fifty-ninth minute, but the goal was ruled offside. The Matildas rallied, dominating possession, and then Elise Kellond-Knight scored from a corner straight into the back of the net in the eighty-third minute. Australia had finally equalised with an amazing 'Olimpico'!

After more than half an hour of extra time, neither team had broken the stalemate and the match headed into a penalty shootout. Norway scored three goals before Australia could sink one. The Matildas were hanging on by the skin of their teeth as Norway readied their fourth shot . . . When the ball hit net, it was all over for the Matildas. Australia was eliminated from the FIFA Women's World Cup 2019™.

Despite their earlier-than-hoped-for elimination, the Matildas had achieved what they'd set out to do – they'd successfully played their style of football and believed in themselves throughout the tournament. It paid off. Australia had the second highest rate of possession of any team in the tournament, and some of the highest percentages for successful passes and crosses.

Individually, Sam Kerr was one of the highest goal scorers of the tournament.

Australia had also left a mark on the international football community as well as the *non*-sporting community worldwide. Suddenly, people knew who the Matildas were – Australia's national women's football team. It was a distinct change from the years where the team were mistaken as everything from volleyballers to hockey players. Not only that, but the Matildas had become one of Australia's most-loved sporting teams.

The FIFA Women's World Cup 2019™ squad

GOALKEEPERS

Lydia Williams
- » Jersey #1
- » Age: 31
- » Home club: Reign FC (USA)

Teagan Micah
- » Jersey #12
- » Age: 21
- » Home club: UCLA (USA)

Mackenzie Arnold
- » Jersey #18
- » Age: 25
- » Home club: Brisbane Roar

DEFENDERS

Gema Simon
- Jersey #2
- Age: 28
- Home club: Newcastle United Jets

Clare Polkinghorne
- Jersey #4
- Age: 30
- Home club: Houston Dash (USA)

Karly Roestbakken
- Jersey #5
- Age: 18
- Home club: Canberra United

Steph Catley
- Jersey #7
- Age: 25
- Home club: Reign FC (USA)

Alanna Kennedy
- Jersey #14
- Age: 24
- Home club: Orlando Pride (USA)

Ellie Carpenter
- Jersey #21
- Age: 19
- Home club: Portland Thorns (USA)

Teigen Allen
- Jersey #23
- Age: 25
- Home club: Melbourne Victory

MIDFIELDERS

Aivi Luik
- Jersey # 3
- Age: 34
- Home club: Levante UD (ESP)

Chloe Logarzo
- Jersey # 6
- Age: 24
- Home club: Washington Spirit (USA)

Elise Kellond-Knight
- Jersey # 8
- Age: 28
- Home club: Reign FC (USA)

Emily van Egmond
- Jersey # 10
- Age: 25
- Home club: Orlando Pride (USA)

Tameka Yallop
- Jersey # 13
- Age: 27
- Home club: Klepp IL (NOR)

Katrina Gorry
- Jersey # 19
- Age: 26
- Home club: Brisbane Roar

Amy Harrison
- Jersey # 22
- Age: 23
- Home club: Sydney FC

FORWARDS

Caitlin Foord
- » Jersey # 9
- » Age: 24
- » Home club: Portland Thorns (USA)

Lisa De Vanna
- » Jersey # 11
- » Age: 34
- » Home club: Sydney FC

Emily Gielnik
- » Jersey # 15
- » Age: 27
- » Home club: Melbourne Victory

Hayley Raso
- » Jersey # 16
- » Age: 24
- » Home club: Portland Thorns (USA)

Mary Fowler
- » Jersey # 17
- » Age: 16
- » Home club: Bankstown City Lions

Sam Kerr – captain
- » Jersey # 20
- » Age: 25
- » Home club: Chicago Red Stars (USA)

SPOTLIGHT

Emily Gielnik

Emily Gielnik wasn't a football player as a kid – she played *basketball* instead! She kept getting injured though, and eventually convinced her parents to let her play football. She made the state team in her very first year as a player, in the Under-12s, and made her senior club debut six years after that. At twenty, she made the Australian national team.

Having now played for the Matildas for a decade, Emily is no stranger to international tournaments. She's made over fifty appearances for Australia, and relishes the opportunities each match brings. She's also played extensively overseas, for clubs like Liverpool, Vittsjö GIK and now Aston Villa.

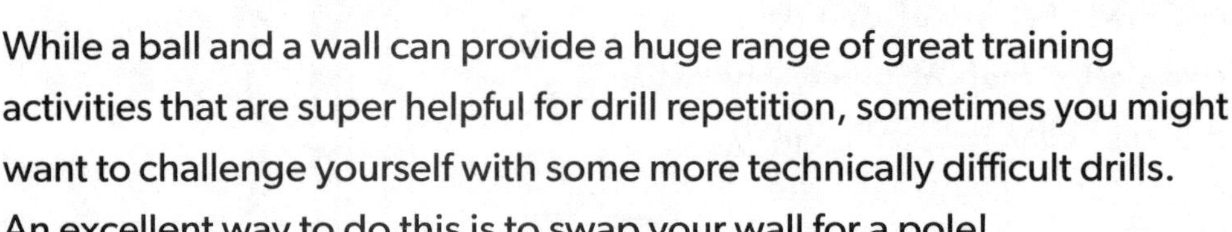

Drills with . . .

A BALL AND A POLE

While a ball and a wall can provide a huge range of great training activities that are super helpful for drill repetition, sometimes you might want to challenge yourself with some more technically difficult drills. An excellent way to do this is to swap your wall for a pole!

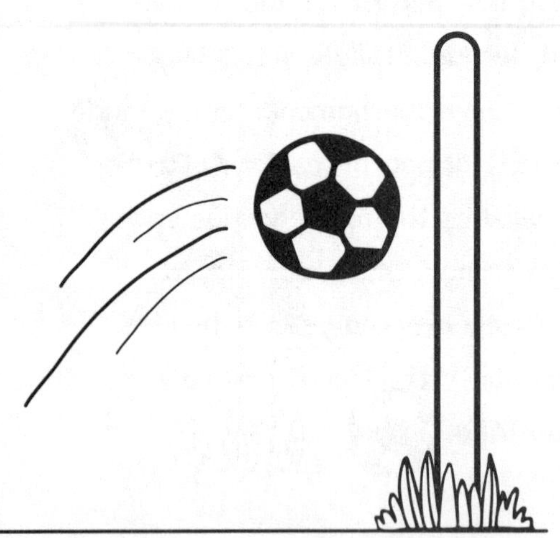

The benefit of a pole is that it's not a wide, flat surface. A ball that's come off another player's foot is very unlikely to behave the same way it would if it came of a wall – a player's foot has heaps of different angles that influence where the ball goes. Poles come in all different sizes, and even different shapes, meaning that there are different surfaces the ball can bounce off. They're a great mimic when you're training on your own!

If you have a backyard with a clothesline or a swing set, you're ready. If not, head to a park. This can be super beneficial even if you *do* have a pole in your backyard. Between play equipment, fence poles or the poles around picnic tables (and more!), parks have plenty of options to vary things up.

Try repeating some of the same drills you used on the wall on your pole – you now have a much smaller area to aim for, which will automatically make the exercises harder. Plus, the pole won't be totally flat. A square or rectangular pole has angled edges that will send the ball flying in unexpected directions if you don't hit the flat part of the pole exactly right.

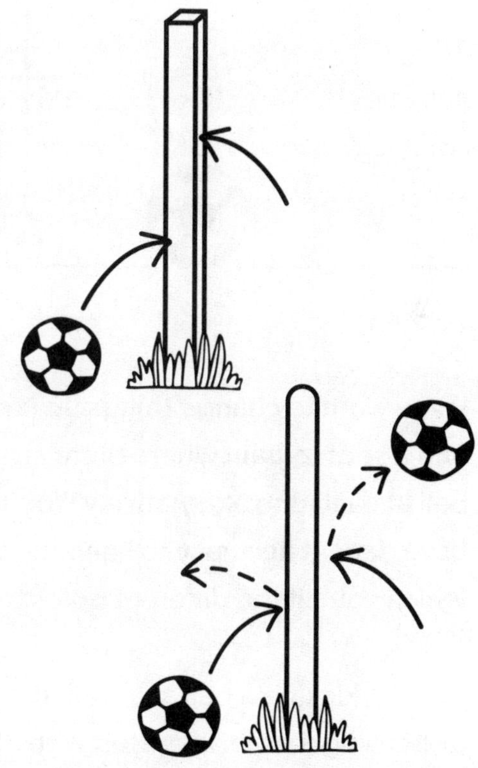

A circular pole is even harder, and thus fantastic to train with. Because it has no flat faces, it's almost impossible to hit the same spot twice – the ball will almost never react the same way two kicks in a row.

The same repetitive drills you used on the wall are great on a pole and you can train your reaction time — and agility — even more as you need to quickly anticipate and move to trap the ball. They're also incredible for your accuracy.

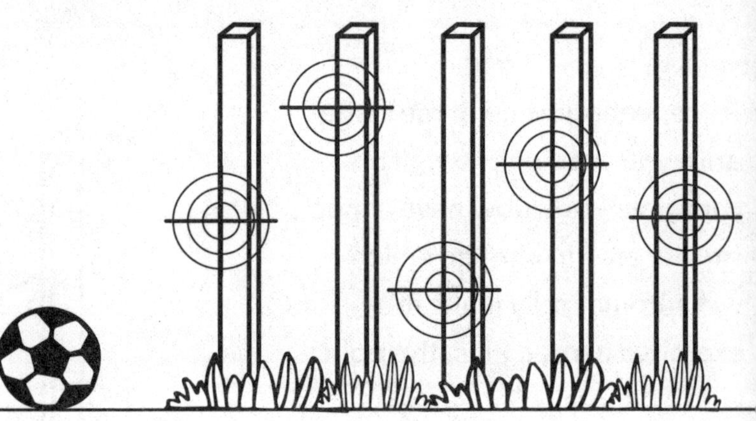

If you want to change things up (and make the drills even harder!), find a spot to train where there are a few poles clustered and kick the ball at each one alternatively. You'll need to be quick on your feet and have decent accuracy to keep the ball moving! Vary up the sequence in which you hit the different poles to keep things interesting.

Just like kicking a ball at a wall, there are so many ways you can differ drills using a pole. Have fun with it!

PLAYING FOR MY

COUNTRY

IS SOMETHING I

NEVER

LET GO OF

-Larissa Crummer-

SPOTLIGHT

Aivi Luik

When Aivi Luik finished school, Australia didn't have a national football league for women. So, in 2003, she made the move to the United States, playing for her university team while she studied for a degree in geography. Then in 2009 (once Australia had started a new national women's league, the W-League) she came back home. Since then, she's divided her time playing for teams in Australia and teams overseas.

In 2010, Aivi was called up to play for the Matildas for the first time, but the road since then has been rocky. She missed out on World Cup and Olympic squads due to performance and injuries for years afterwards. Then she was selected for the FIFA Women's World Cup 2019™ squad and made her World Cup debut in the eighty-seventh minute of Australia's game against Jamaica. She was thirty-four years old. It was an emotional time, and she later said she'd go through all the hard parts of her career again just to have those minutes.

In 2021, she got to play for the Matildas in a major tournament once more, appearing in three Olympic matches. After Tokyo, Aivi announced her retirement from international football. She wasn't retired for long though. At thirty-six, she was called up to the squad for the 2022 AFC Women's Asian Cup.

Her amazing career has led her to be the oldest-ever footballer to play for the Matildas – a testament to her skills as well as her character, experience and attitude. She's a mentor and role model for younger players – just as important off the field as she is on it.

Stories and Advice from the ParaMatildas

What's your favourite junior footballing memory?

As a young kid, I wasn't involved in a football team. There weren't many football programs available for disabled kids, especially not in rural areas, and there was no pathway to pursue it as a career, but I always loved the sport and used to play 'backyard' football in our paddock at home.

Kids from around the street would all gather for the games, and would begin inviting their own friends too. Everyone was welcome and everyone loved it. We made goals out of logs, garbage bins, or anything else we could find, and eventually saved up for some cones to mark out the lines.

We didn't have boots, or uniforms, but it was the highlight of every weekend and played a massive part in my passion for football now.

- Tahlia Blanshard

FRIENDS FOR LIFE

When you play competitive sport, you tend to start coming up against the same athletes again and again. That's how Alanna Kennedy and Caitlin Foord first met.

They were rivals at Little Athletics from age seven. Alanna was better at jumping – she held records in long jump, high jump and hurdles – while Caitlin was a sprinter. Then, one day, Caitlin saw Alanna somewhere unexpected: a school football competition. Here was her running rival, now stepping on her football turf!

But, as the years progressed, the girls found themselves appearing more and more in each other's orbits until they were attending Matildas training camps together. That's where they met Mackenzie Arnold. Now, the three have been best friends for years.

Alanna, Caitlin and Mackenzie say that having your best friends with you on your football journey with you is like nothing else. The trio can have fun anywhere, which comes in handy during training camps when they need to unwind from long days of thinking, living and breathing football.

They're also super proud of each other's achievements, celebrating the big and little moments together. But it's what happens off the field that makes the friendship between players so special – having your teammates to turn to in the tough times, even when you're not together.

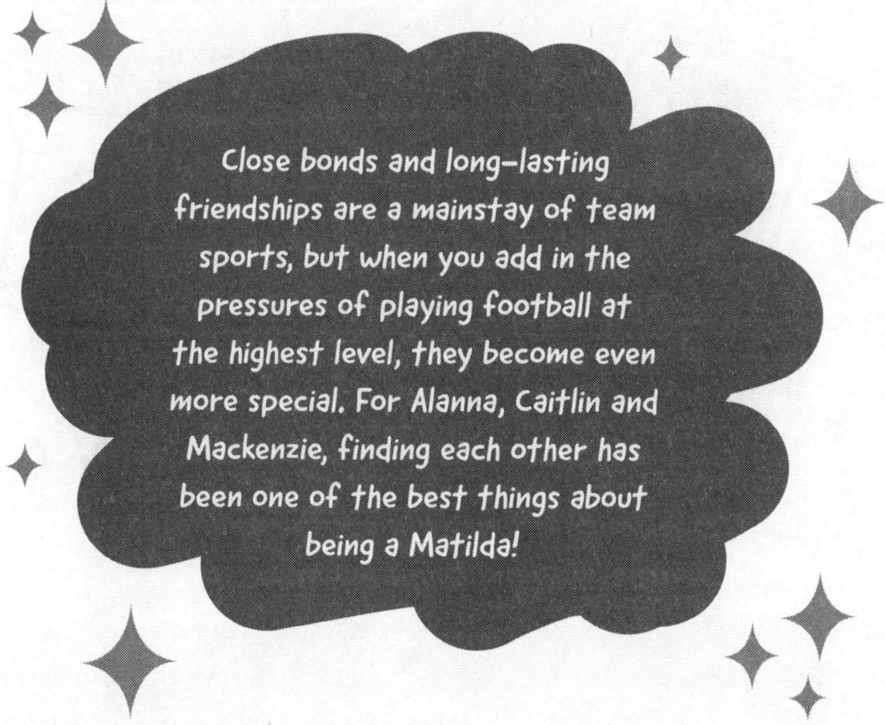

SPOTLIGHT

Mackenzie Arnold

Mackenzie Arnold is one of Australia's best goalkeepers. Her fearlessness helps her achieve a super-high efficiency in goals that has seen her play club football all over the globe, and she's even been approached to join a professional AFL team!
Her consistency and quick-reaction saves don't hurt, either.

Mackenzie spent nine years playing in the W-League – and was recognised as Goalkeeper of the Year three times – before making the permanent move overseas to play for West Ham United in England's Women's Super League.

As one of the Matildas' goalkeepers, Mackenzie has played more than two-dozen matches and racked up over ten clean sheets. It's an impressive ratio that makes her one of the country's most successful goalies.

The 2020 Tokyo Olympics

The qualifying tournament for the 2020 Tokyo Olympic Games started in Malaysia in 2018. As one of the top-ranked teams in the world, however, the Matildas had been allowed to bypass early qualifying rounds and compete only at the very last stage of qualifiers, in February 2020.

At the time of the tournament, the COVID-19 pandemic was just starting to become known to the world. The matches – originally intended to be held in China – were moved to Australia. The Matildas faced Chinese Taipei, Thailand and China PR in their group, winning the first two matches and drawing the last to finish at the top of their round.

Playoff matches were held across multiple countries, with the Matildas competing on both home soil and in Myanmar in early March for the chance to play at the Olympics. They won both of their matches, qualifying alongside China PR and Olympic hosts Japan for Tokyo 2020.

Then, on the same day the Matildas qualified, the World Health Organisation declared that the COVID-19 outbreak was a global pandemic and the Summer Olympics was postponed to 2021.

When Australia finally made it to Japan, they found a very different Olympic experience. At Rio in 2016, they had competed in front of crowds of more than 52,000 people. In 2021, the stadiums were utterly empty.

Another complication was that, due to the pandemic and Australian government regulations, the Matildas had barely managed to train as a team in the lead up to the Games, let alone play in many preparation matches. Plus, while Tony Gustavsson had officially been the team's head coach for a year, he'd spent most of that time stuck in Sweden due to the Australian government's strict border closure.

It wasn't until just over three months out from the Olympics that the team was finally able to play some friendlies against the Netherlands, Germany, Denmark, Japan and Sweden. The Matildas struggled to pull together at first, but quickly managed to start shoring up their defence. They'd grown a lot as a team, but was it enough to put them into contention for an Olympic medal?

The tournament was tricky from the start. Australia were drawn in a group with the United States, Sweden and New Zealand, facing off against two of the top-five teams for a chance to advance to the knockouts.

Up first was New Zealand. Goals by Tameka Yallop and Sam Kerr in the first half secured Australia's win, with the Kiwis unable to equalise despite a late-minute goal in extra time. Next up, Matildas faced Sweden. More than 1.87 million Australians tuned in to watch the game – a record for women's sport in Australia. Unfortunately, the game was a dramatic 2–4 loss for the Matildas.

Australia played well in their last group match, dominating possession against the world number one. Both the Australian and USA teams had attempts at goals but were unable to convert, resulting in a 0–0 draw. The Matildas finished the group stage with four points – not as many as they'd wanted, but enough to progress to the knockout games.

The Matildas faced Great Britain in the quarter-final. A goal by Alanna Kennedy in the thirty-fifth minute put Australia ahead going into the half. Great Britain equalised, then pulled ahead with two goals in the second half. The Matildas' chance at a semi-final spot looked all but over until a goal by Kerr in the second-last minute of the match impossibly sent the game into extra time! Mary Fowler brought Australia ahead with a goal in her first-ever Olympic Games, and Kerr cemented it with her second. Despite a third goal for Great Britain, the game ended 4–3 in Australia's favour.

The Matildas had done it - they'd surpassed their previous performances and were through to an Olympic semi-final!

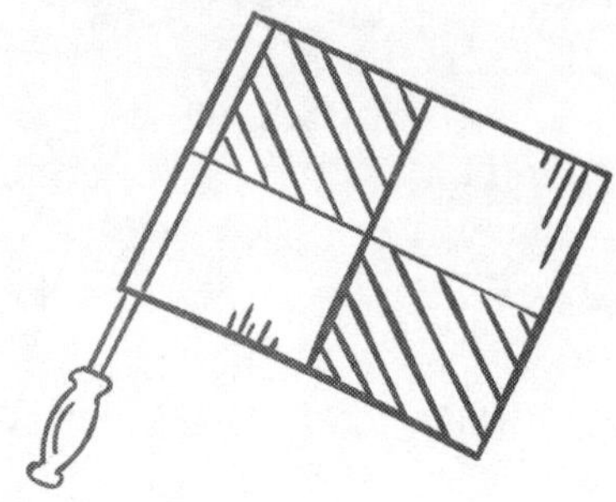

Competing for an Olympic gold had been the Matildas' dream, and yet it wasn't to be. In the semi, the team faced Sweden for the second time in the Games. Australia pushed hard in the first half, dominating possession and putting the pressure on Sweden before Sam Kerr sunk the ball into the back of the net in the forty-second minute. The Matildas barely got to celebrate before the devastating news came through – the goal had been disallowed. One of the Australian players had been offside and impeded the Swedish defenders.

The Matildas did their best to score again but were unable to push through. Sweden sunk a goal in the seventy-fourth minute and the Australians were unable to equalise. The game ended 0–1. The Matildas were out of contention for gold or silver, but there was still one more match to play: the game for third against the mighty USA.

The bronze-medal match was held three days later. The USA scored quickly to take the lead, but Sam Kerr equalised less than ten minutes later with a goal that landed her the title of the Matildas' all-time top scorer at forty-eight goals for Australia. The opposition scored another two goals before the half, and the teams headed into the break 1–3 to the USA. The USA scored again quickly in the second half, but their lead was soon shortened by Caitlin Foord, who landed a goal in the fifty-fourth minute. A third Australian goal was netted by Emily

Gielnik in the ninetieth minute, but the Matildas were ultimately unable to equalise. The match finished 3–4 to the USA.

Australia had narrowly missed out on a medal, but had their best-ever performance at an Olympic Games. They'd had a historic fourth-place finish and reached their very first major tournament semi-final. And Sam Kerr had one of the highest goal counts of the Games for both the men's and women's competition too. The Matildas' 'Never Say Die' attitude and passion had captivated Australia and made the team the most-watched women's sports team in Australian television history.

It had been a phenomenal campaign by the Matildas, and Australia couldn't have been prouder.

The 2020 Summer Olympics squad

GOALKEEPERS

Lydia Williams
- Jersey #1
- Age: 33
- Home club: Arsenal (ENG)

Teagan Micah
- Jersey #18
- Age: 23
- Home club: IL Sandviken (NOR)

Mackenzie Arnold
- Jersey #22
- Age: 27
- Home club: West Ham (ENG)

DEFENDERS

Clare Polkinghorne
- Jersey #4
- Age: 32
- Home club: Vittsjö GIK (SWE)

Aivi Luik
- Jersey #5
- Age: 36
- Home club: Sevilla (ESP)

Steph Catley
- Jersey #7
- Age: 27
- Home club: Arsenal (ENG)

Ellie Carpenter
- Jersey #12
- Age: 21
- Home club: Olympique Lyon (FRA)

Alanna Kennedy
- Jersey #14
- Age: 26
- Home club: Tottenham Hotspur (ENG)
- Agent

Courtney Nevin
- Jersey #19
- Age: 19
- Home club: Western Sydney Wanderers

Charlotte Grant
- Jersey #20
- Age: 19
- Home club: FC Rosengård (SWE)

Laura Brock
- Jersey #21
- Age: 31
- Home club: EA Guingamp (FRA)

MIDFIELDERS

Kyra Cooney-Cross
» Jersey #3
» Age: 19
» Home club: Melbourne Victory

Chloe Logarzo
» Jersey #6
» Age: 26
» Home club: Kansas City (USA)

Elise Kellond-Knight
» Jersey #8
» Age: 30
» Home club: Hammarby (SWE)

Emily van Egmond
» Jersey #10
» Age: 27
» Home club: West Ham (ENG)

Tameka Yallop
» Jersey #13
» Age: 30
» Home club: West Ham (ENG)

FORWARDS

Sam Kerr – captain

- Jersey #2
- Age: 27
- Home club: Chelsea (ENG)

Caitlin Foord

- Jersey #9
- Age: 26
- Home club: Arsenal (ENG)

Mary Fowler

- Jersey #11
- Age: 18
- Home club: Montpellier (FRA)

Emily Gielnik

- Jersey #15
- Age: 29
- Home club: Brisbane Roar

Hayley Raso

- Jersey #16
- Age: 26
- Home club: Everton (ENG)

Kyah Simon

- Jersey #17
- Age: 30
- Home club: PSV Vrouwen (NLD)

SPOTLIGHT

Mary Fowler

When Mary Fowler made her debut for the Matildas in 2018, she was the first player in a long time to walk onto the field for the national team before making her club senior debut.

Mary's childhood was spent playing beach Olympics with her family, kicking a ball around after school day-in, day-out. She got so good that when she joined the Queensland state team at ten years old, she played with her older sister for the Under-12s. Her older brother says she lived and breathed football, training before and after school on her own before heading out to club practice.

Mary's whole family moved to Europe when she was eleven, following the career of her older brother. She spent the next few years honing her skills there. Though she seems to have come from nowhere, her rise to the top of Australian football is the product of years of hard work and dedication. Mary is always thinking about what she needs to do to improve her game, and she focuses on the smaller time frames, letting each month of training build across time to make her an even better player. Now, years after those beach Olympics days, she's played multiple tournaments for the Matildas . . . including stepping onto the field and coming full circle in the 2020 Tokyo Olympic Games.

The Impact of Injury

Injuries are some of the most devastating things a footballer can endure, keeping them from playing the game they love and representing their team.

Injuries can be small, like bruises and strains, or have longer impacts like fractures and dislocations. The worst injuries can threaten a player's career completely – torn ACLs and broken bones.

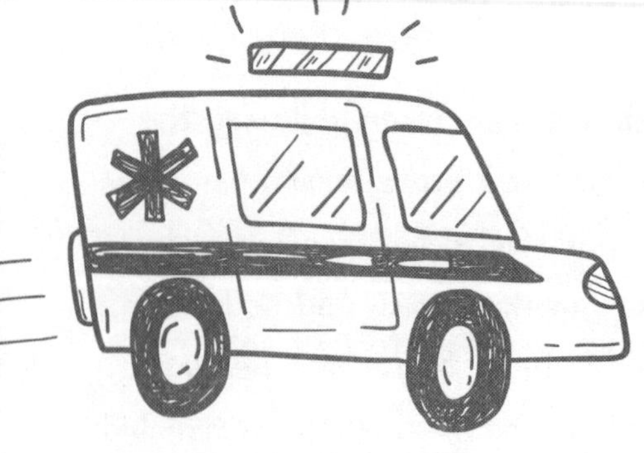

The Matildas are no strangers to injuries. When Laura Alleway (now Laura Brock) injured her foot the day before the FIFA Women's World Cup 2019™ began, she was forced to spend the tournament in the stands, cheering her teammates to their eventual knockout in the round of 16. In 2021, Chloe Logarzo tore her ACL during a Matildas friendly, forcing her into months of recovery. In 2022, Ellie Carpenter suffered

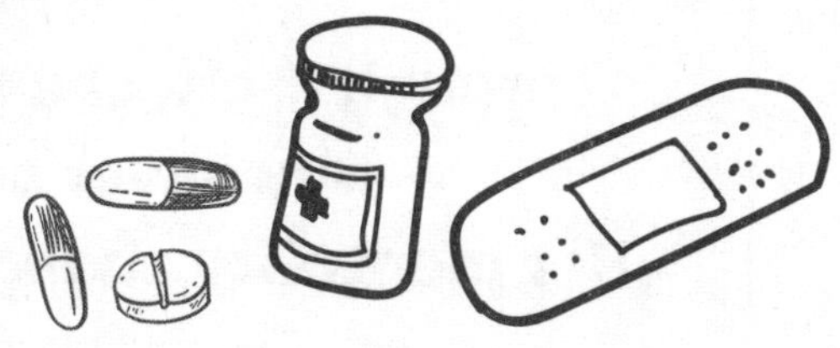

the same injury while playing the UEFA Champion's League final for her home club, Olympique Lyon – now she's racing against time to be healed and ready to play for the Matildas on home soil in the FIFA Women's World Cup 2023™.

Almost every player has tales of injuries that kept them sidelined for months, impacting not only their fitness and ability to play the game, but also their mentality. It's moments like these that the support of the community and the 'Never Say Die' motto come into full force.

Sam Kerr has described her major injuries as the lowest points in her life, and Steph Catley called her injury-plagued first season with Arsenal the hardest of her career so far. But, as the players' bodies began to heal, they turned to the people around them to help regain not just their technical skills but their love of the game and an attitude that has made them even better athletes.

One of the most incredible recovery stories on the team is Hayley Raso's. In 2018, in a match for her then-home club Portland Thorns, Hayley got a knee to her back that fractured three vertebrae and left her legs completely numb. She didn't know if she'd ever walk again, let alone play football – and forget about playing for the national team. Months of rehabilitation helped Hayley relearn how to walk again. Then her old coach at Brisbane Roar invited her to come and train with the team. Incredibly, she soon returned to the field and has been back with the Matildas squad since 2019.

Through it all, she never gave up.
She never said die.
Her mentality changed everything.

Playing professional football does carry a lot of risk of injury, but thankfully the vast majority of injuries are nowhere near as severe as the ones described above. Plus, a lot of injuries can be minimised or prevented as players improve their skills and knowledge of the game.

Being fit and practising good technique all help reduce the risk of injury. The Matildas spend time developing and improving their endurance, coordination, flexibility, strength and balance to ensure their bodies are ready to meet the demands of football. Not even playing for the national team means footballers can stop practising the basics to make sure they know how to do it properly and safely. And they always remember to warm up!

Warming up applies to training loads as well. It's important to build up to an intensive load slowly over time. Making sure they give their bodies time to adapt ensures players create endurance and robustness. Building the physical load too quickly risks overtraining and burnout. Training sessions in the gym to build strength, as well as sessions focusing on mobility, are just as important as practising techniques.

Another thing the Matildas do to avoid injuries is to have a people-first approach. It's something that coach Tony Gustavsson calls meeting players where they are as individuals – with compassion for events happening in their life outside the team – rather than thinking of them only as footballers. It means that players are rotated regularly during tournaments and games to ensure every player receives both the pitch time and the rest they need. It also means finding opportunities for players returning from injuries to get back on the field at their own pace – incrementally, rather than all at once – while they rebuild their skills, fitness and confidence.

Injuries can have big impacts on a player's fitness or even career, but putting in the effort to minimise the risk of injury (and keeping a positive attitude if it does happen) can help!

Practising kicking and receiving the ball are great ways to train a lot of skills at once, but there are plenty of exercises you can do to improve things like your footwork, agility, precision and more. Juggling the ball with your feet is a great one – plus it doesn't require nearly as much space, and even less 'equipment' than the ball and a wall or pole drills. All you need is a ball and your feet!

Start with basic juggling – how many times can you kick the ball up without it hitting the ground? Keeping the ball on the move in the same small space is harder than it seems!

The variations you can introduce to the exercise are practically endless though – all you need to do is impose rules.

How many times can you successfully juggle the ball . . .

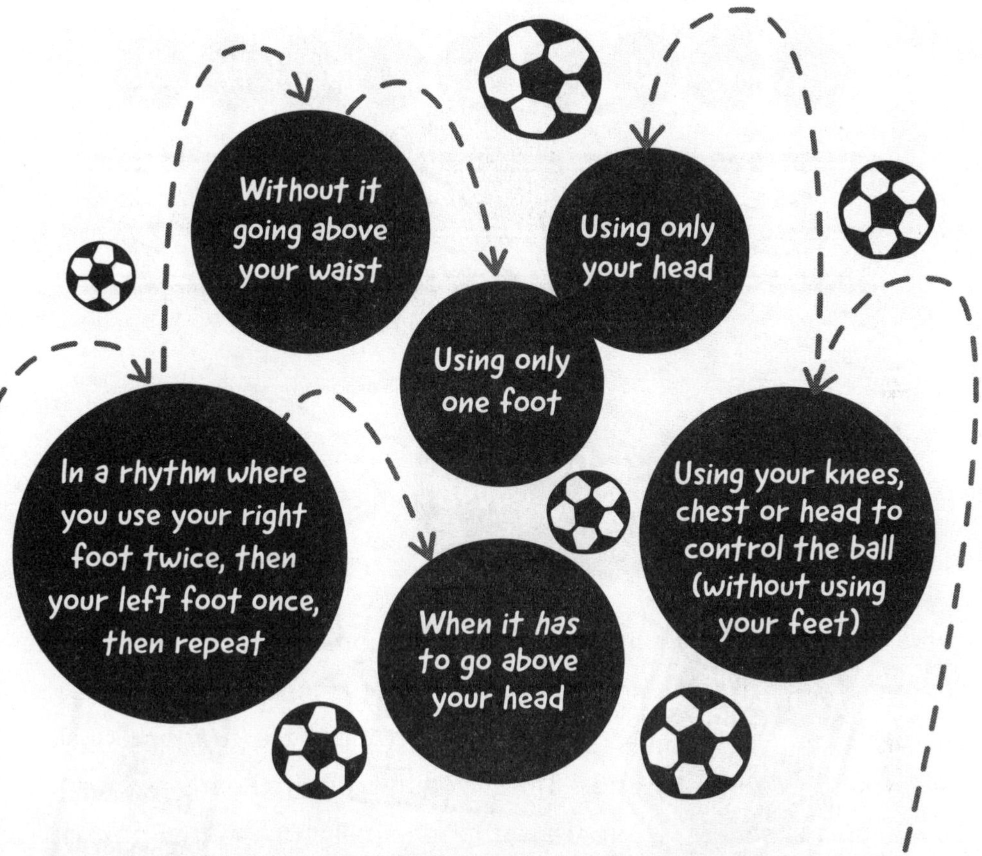

And, of course, you can integrate juggling into other drills. Maybe you have to juggle the ball eight times, then kick it and hit a certain spot on the wall, trap it and start juggling again. Or you could do it with a partner – juggle for a minute then pass to each other and repeat!

How many other variations and challenges can you think of?

SPOTLIGHT

Larissa Crummer

When Larissa Crummer debuted for Sydney FC at sixteen, it was clear she had a bright footballing future ahead of her. She quickly became a regular starter of the W-League, receiving both Golden Boot and Young Player of the Year awards for the 2015-16 season. By this point, she'd been playing for the Young Matildas side for a few years, and had recently received her senior Matildas call-up. Larissa played the FIFA Women's World Cup 2015™ and the 2016 Rio Olympics, and looked set to join the squad for the FIFA Women's World Cup 2019™ in France when disaster struck.

In January 2019, Larissa was playing a club match for Newcastle Jets when she shattered both the tibia and fibula in her left leg after a nasty collision on the field. Then, problems during surgery meant Larissa had to undergo surgery again and again to ensure she didn't lose her leg. She worked hard on rehabilitation after her injuries, training with Brisbane Roar to sharpen her skills and fitness before returning to the team full-time in 2021.

She's since reappeared for the Matildas too, and is keen to start right where she left off: angling for a spot on the World Cup squad.

The Matildas on . . .

BEING CALLED UP TO THE WORLD CUP

Being called up to a World Cup squad is one of the greatest honours a Matilda can have – to represent your country, inspire the next generation, showcase what a Matilda can do and help the game evolve . . . and of course potentially hold up the ultimate prize with your football family!

EVER WONDERED WHAT THE CALL-UP FEELS LIKE?

I was really excited, but . . . I always **believed** I was going to be a Matilda.

Lisa De Vanna

The feeling's kind of **indescribable**. It's everything you've ever worked for and everything you've ever **dreamed of**.

Tameka Yallop

There's a huge sense of **pride.** It's an unbelievable feeling.

Sam Kerr

I was **excited** out of my *skin*.

Laura Brock

I was extremely excited, very **proud** and looking forward to the **opportunity to represent my country** on the *biggest stage* for football.

Alanna Kennedy

The **best days of my life** are getting the news that you've made a World Cup squad and you're heading to a World Cup.

Clare Polkinghorne

It **meant the world** to me. It was pretty exciting, pretty nerve-racking.

Lydia Williams

I got the call only a couple of days before we went into the camp. It was a very proud moment for myself and my family. **I'll never forget that.**

Mackenzie Arnold

I was just excited to **represent my family** after they'd done so much for me. I definitely wouldn't be where I am today and I wouldn't have had that chance if they didn't sacrifice so much for me when I was younger.

Gema Simon

SPOTLIGHT

Alex Chidiac

When Alex Chidiac made her professional debut for Adelaide United at fifteen, she was already an accomplished player, having appeared for both the Junior and Young Matildas, the South Australian Under-14/15 team and receiving the Player of the Tournament award at Australia's National Youth Championships when she was just fourteen.

Alex had already travelled to three international tournaments with the senior Matildas by the time she turned twenty, and played in several friendly matches.

She's known for her sure footing and inventive attack – a style of play that has seen her represent clubs in Japan, Spain and now the USA.

The bid for the FIFA Women's World Cup 2023™

In 2017, the Matildas were one of Australia's most-loved sporting teams. They were ranked eighth in the world, and the Australian government wanted to capitalise on the increasing profile of women's sport in Australia to encourage and inspire even more girls and young women to have a go.

So the government (along with Football Federation Australia) started thinking about whether they'd be able to bring the FIFA Women's World Cup 2023™ to Australia. By 2018 they were sure they could make it happen. Australia's bid to host was officially launched to the public in October.

The Matildas were beyond excited to potentially play a World Cup on home soil and cement the support and development of women's sport in Australia. They encouraged all Australians to register support

and get behind the bid to show FIFA just how much the country cared about hosting such an important event.

A few months later, in February 2019, FIFA opened the bidding for the 2023 Women's World Cup. Nine countries said they were interested, including both Australia and New Zealand, which was the largest number to ever volunteer to host the women's event.

Both Australia and New Zealand campaigned hard for the opportunity. New Zealand had just held the men's Under-20 World Cup, while Australia was investing in brand new facilities and proudly showcasing our history of hosting world-class sporting events (including the 2000 Olympics and the men's 2015 AFC Asian Cup).

Before the bidding deadline closed, FIFA announced an increase in the number of qualifying finalists from twenty-four to thirty-two teams. This had an impact on the capacity to host an event with thirty-two teams and hence Australia and New Zealand decided to put in the joint bid, sharing the responsibilities and the love of the game. It was the first-ever co-host bid between countries from two different football confederations (Asia for Australia, and Oceania for New Zealand). If the combined bid, called #AsOne, was to win hosting rights, then the FIFA Women's World Cup 2023™ would also be the first to be held in the Southern Hemisphere.

The #AsOne bid was up against some stiff competition. Colombia, Japan and Brazil had also submitted bids.

After the bids were submitted, FIFA took six months to evaluate the options they'd been presented. In June, it was announced that the Australia-New Zealand bid was the highest quality option. Things were looking positive for the #AsOne bid! It wasn't over yet though. Two weeks later, after considering the evaluation results, the FIFA council held a vote to choose who would host the FIFA Women's World Cup 2023™.

At this point, Japan and Brazil had withdrawn their bids, so the final vote was just between two options - Australia-New Zealand and Colombia.

A number of Matildas came together in Sydney to await the announcement. Because of the time differences between Australia and FIFA headquarters, the result wasn't going to be known until 1 am on June 26. Despite this, with all of Australia invested in the outcome, players were up early on June 25 to talk to the media. Excitement was high – especially for Kyah Simon. The announcement was coming through on her birthday!

At 5:30 pm, there were still more than seven hours until the announcement – the Matildas were in for a long night. There was one more big event – watching the Sydney Opera House light up with photographs of the team, including past players like Julie Dolan, cap number one, who had played in the first-ever international game against New Zealand in 1979.

Eventually, everyone gathered at Football Australia headquarters. The team continued talking to the general public with TV appearances and Facebook lives, keeping the buzz going as the night went on. Then – finally – it was almost time. Just after 1 am, players from the Matildas and the New Zealand Football Ferns met with key members of Football Australia and New Zealand Football to make a video call to FIFA headquarters.

At 1:40 am, the result came through. The room exploded with noise when Australia and New Zealand #AsOne was announced as the winning bid.

For the first time, two countries from two different FIFA confederations would be the official hosts of the FIFA Women's World Cup™!

In July and August 2023, thirty-two teams from six confederations will come to play in stadiums across both countries, with venues in Adelaide, Brisbane, Melbourne, Perth, Sydney, Auckland, Dunedin, Hamilton and Wellington. Football Australia and New Zealand Football have committed to celebrating the women's game in the best way they know how with a player-focused tournament, and the Matildas see the win as a fantastic opportunity to inspire a whole new generation of female footballers in Australia.

The FIFA Women's World Cup is the largest women's sporting event in the world. To be the hosts of the competition is the ultimate honour for the footballing community, and the co-hosting relationship across Australia and New Zealand as well as Asia and Oceania confederations shows just how supportive that community is of each other and of women's football.

To be co-hosting the World Cup is the pinnacle of women's football in Australia so far, and a true endorsement of just how far the Matildas have come since their first international tournament all those decades ago.

"I really genuinely believe this team can do amazing things"

Tony Gustavsson

SPOTLIGHT

Kyra Cooney-Cross

Despite only making her debut a couple of years ago, Kyra Cooney-Cross has already appeared more than fifteen times for the Matildas. She's a super versatile player, which means she's a favoured substitute during top-level matches – a skill that saw her coming on in all six of Australia's games at the 2020 Olympics, and that has meant she's regularly called up to the Matildas squad.

Though she's clearly a great player, Kyra still struggles with nerves when she first steps on the field, scared to stuff up and disappoint the team. She doesn't let the nerves stop her though, and her performance has caught the eye of coaches the world over! She signed with Swedish team Hammarby IF in 2022 after five seasons in the Australian A-League Women, playing for Melbourne Victory and the Western Sydney Wanderers.

If you have a bit more space and equipment (or even just a space full of stuff), why not put a bunch of skills together by setting yourself an obstacle course?

There are lots of different ways you could train on an obstacle course . . .

- Run without a ball to hone in on agility, speed and fitness.
- Pretend each obstacle is a defender and dribble your way around the course, practising your fast turns to run rings around each cone, pole – or whatever your obstacles are.
- Incorporate shooting into your obstacle course. Maybe you can dribble around a handful of defenders before getting your chance to hit a target on a wall?
- Incorporate passing into your drill by dribbling around pretend defenders before passing to the wall, controlling the ball and heading back the way you came. Passing to poles would make this even harder!

Obstacles can be created with anything you have on hand. Maybe it's cones, or play equipment or maybe it's discarded shoes or jumpers. Maybe it's even buildings or involves vertical changes like moving from a grassed backyard to a short deck. If it helps you improve your skills on the ball, it's good!

What about a drill where you complete circuits of a space, alternating between different types of dribbling (for example, passing super-quickly back and forward between your feet while you move forward slowly versus the kind of dribbling where you take two strides between ball touches) and stopping to juggle every twenty metres?

WHAT OTHER EXERCISES COULD YOU COMBINE?

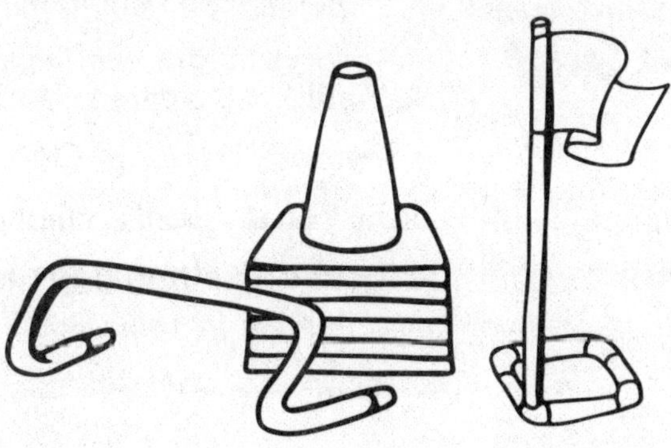

WHAT MAKES A MATILDA

While technical skills and performance on the field is an important part of what makes a Matilda, the qualities that someone has off the pitch are super important too.

A Matilda is someone who's passionate about football, who has a love for the game. If you have a football-shaped fire inside, you already have one of the most important qualities of a Matilda!

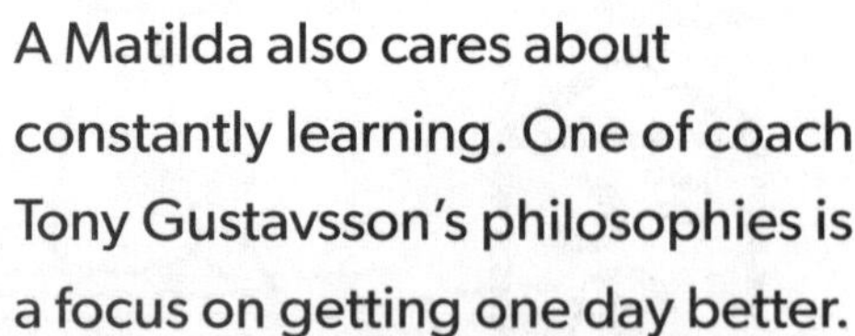

A Matilda also cares about constantly learning. One of coach Tony Gustavsson's philosophies is a focus on getting one day better.

A Matilda is someone who strives to improve their technical skills, their physical ability, their mental game – just a little bit – every day.

A Matilda is someone who believes in the potential of themselves and their team while meeting themselves where they are at the time. If they're recovering from injury, they're not going to expect themselves to be able to play a full game perfectly! But they do believe that they'll get there.

A Matilda gives back to the community that helped them get to where they are today, making things even better for the next generation of footballers and the women and girls who will come after them.

A Matilda is someone who is proud to play for their country and show the world exactly what Australian footballers are made of.

A Matilda is ready to fight hard to beat the odds. They have the toughness to stick out the journey, no matter what life throws at them. They have the ambition and hunger to succeed!

A Matilda is someone who listens to their coaches and follows instructions. They can accept criticism and turn it into real improvements in their game, as well as taking responsibility for their mistakes.

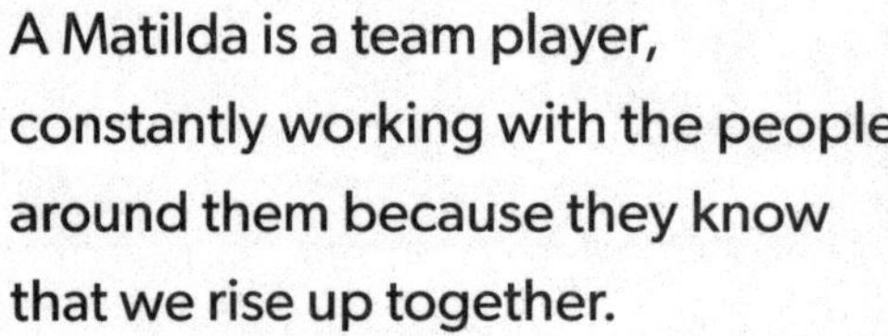

A Matilda is a team player, constantly working with the people around them because they know that we rise up together.

A Matilda is someone who works hard outside of their training sessions – they're a self-starter who finds opportunities to work on their skills at home.

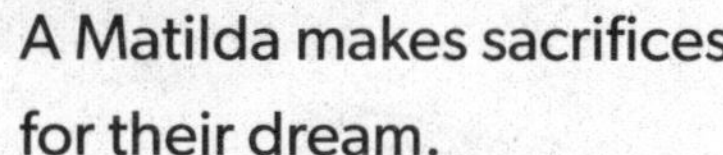

A Matilda makes sacrifices for their dream.

And a Matilda
never gives up!

SPOTLIGHT

Courtney Nevin

Courtney Nevin's career for the Matildas began long before she made her senior team debut. By the time that happened, she'd already been playing for the Junior and Young Matildas since she was fourteen. She made her senior club debut two years later, for the Western Sydney Wanderers.

Though she plays at full-back, Courtney's known for her killer technique on the ball and has scored several goals for Australia at the youth level.

Her first senior international call-up came during her Higher School Certificate, but she didn't make her official debut until two years later, playing in two friendlies before becoming an Olympian. Courtney's made several appearances for the Matildas since then, and has made the move to Sweden to improve her game and help secure consistent appointments to the Australian team.

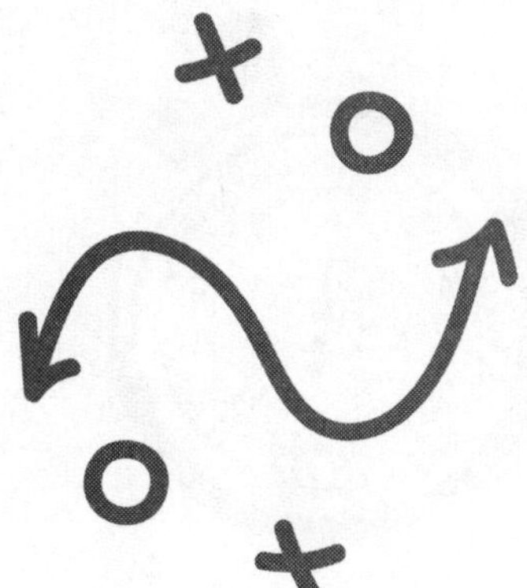

The 2022 Asian Cup

The 2022 AFC Women's Asian Cup was the twentieth edition of the cup, and the eighth the Matildas had attended. Australia went into the competition having already automatically qualified for the FIFA Women's World Cup 2023™ as a co-host country.

Like the 2020 Tokyo Olympics, the 2022 Asian Cup was held without crowds in the stands. Australia faced Indonesia, the Philippines and Thailand in the group stage feeling more prepared than they had for the Games the year before.

The first group game was against Indonesia, and the Matildas led from the start, ultimately finishing the game 18–0. It was a big game for more than just the Matildas as a team. Scoring five of Australia's goals during the match, Sam Kerr became the country's greatest ever goal scorer, overtaking previous record holder Tim Cahill with fifty-four goals for Australia since her national team debut in the 2010 Asian Cup at just sixteen years old.

Next up was the Philippines. There was a deadlock for the entire first half. The Matildas had trouble breaking through the Philippines' defence and just couldn't convert their opportunities on goal until the fifty-first minute with a goal by Kerr. An own-goal by the Philippines followed before Emily van Egmond and Mary Fowler scored in the sixty-seventh and eighty-seventh minutes respectively with the game ending 4–0.

Australia's final group match against Thailand was something of a redemption for the Matildas, with the team playing a smoother game. Despite Australia's dominance with possession and attempts on goal, Thailand's defence was strong. The score was 1–0 to Australia going into half-time thanks to a thirty-ninth minute goal from Van Egmond. The second half yielded little extra ground until the eightieth minute, when Kerr scored her seventh goal of the tournament. Thailand narrowed the gap during extra time, but were unable to equalise. The game ended 2–1, and the Matildas were through to the knockout stage.

The Matildas faced South Korea in the quarter-final – a team they'd played almost twenty times before, with Australia winning most of those matches. Both teams were coming off a stream of victories and plenty to play for. Australia had qualified at the top of their group with nine points to South Korea's seven.

The match was easily the most exciting quarter-final in the tournament as Australia and South Korea each fought for dominance. Australia continually pushed forward only to be stopped by the South Korean defence. The Matildas just couldn't convert their opportunities on goal, and the score remained 0–0 well into the second half. Then, just thirteen minutes out from full-time, the worst happened for Australia's hopes of another Asian Cup final. South Korea struck from outside the box and the ball found the top corner of the net. The Matildas fought on but still couldn't capitalise on their chances and the game ended 0–1.

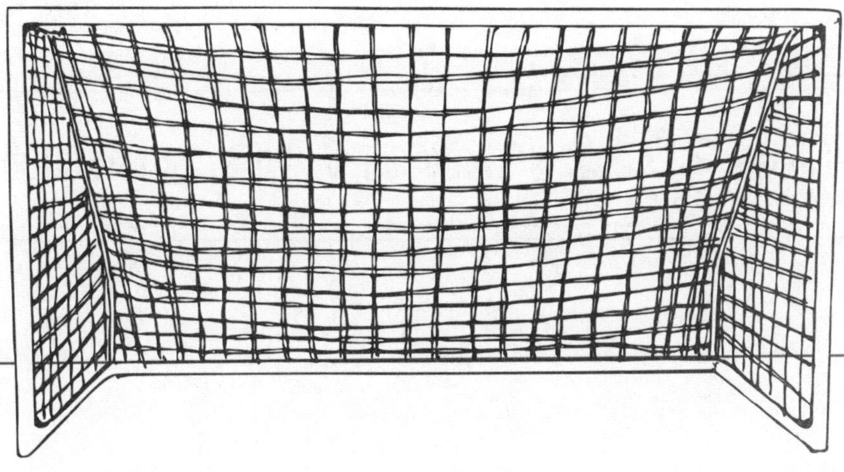

It was a bittersweet loss for the Matildas, who had never placed below fourth in the tournament. To be knocked out in the quarter-final was a devastating blow for a team who, despite their wins in the group stage, had not played as well as they'd known they could throughout the entire Asian Cup.

But, as hosts of the 2023 FIFA Women's World Cup, they had qualified for the upcoming tournament regardless - and would soon be playing the world's largest women's football tournament on home soil.

The 2022 Asian Cup squad

GOALKEEPERS

Lydia Williams
- Jersey #1
- Age: 33
- Home club: Arsenal (ENG)

Teagan Micah
- Jersey #12
- Age: 24
- Home club: FC Rosengård (SWE)

Mackenzie Arnold
- Jersey #18
- Age: 27
- Home club: West Ham United (ENG)

DEFENDERS

Courtney Nevin
- Jersey #2
- Age: 19
- Home club: Melbourne Victory

Clare Polkinghorne
- Jersey #4
- Age: 32
- Home club: Vittsjö GIK (SWE)

Steph Catley
- Jersey #7
- Age: 27
- Home club: Arsenal (ENG)

Charlotte Grant
- Jersey #8
- Age: 20
- Home club: FC Rosengård (SWE)

Alanna Kennedy
- Jersey #14
- Age: 26
- Home club: Manchester City (ENG)

Ellie Carpenter
- Jersey #21
- Age: 21
- Home club: Lyon (FRA)

MIDFIELDERS

Aivi Luik
- » Jersey #3
- » Age: 36
- » Home club: Pomigliano (ITA)

Clare Wheeler
- » Jersey #6
- » Age: 24
- » Home club: Fortuna Hjørring (DNK)

Emily van Egmond
- » Jersey #10
- » Age: 28
- » Home club: Newcastle Jets

Tameka Yallop
- » Jersey #13
- » Age: 30
- » Home club: West Ham United (ENG)

FORWARDS

Cortnee Vine

- Jersey #5
- Age: 23
- Home club: Sydney FC

Caitlin Foord

- Jersey #9
- Age: 27
- Home club: Arsenal (ENG)

Mary Fowler

- Jersey #11
- Age: 18
- Home club: Montpellier (FRA)

Emily Gielnik

- Jersey #15
- Age: 29
- Home club: Aston Villa (ENG)

Hayley Raso

- Jersey #16
- Age: 27
- Home club: Manchester City (ENG)

Kyah Simon

- Jersey #17
- Age: 30
- Home club: Tottenham Hotspur (ENG)

FORWARDS

Kyra Cooney-Cross

- Jersey #19
- Age: 19
- Home club: Melbourne Victory

Sam Kerr – captain

- Jersey #20
- Age: 28
- Home club: Chelsea (ENG)

Holly McNamara

- Jersey #22
- Age: 18
- Home club: Melbourne City

Remy Siemsen

- Jersey #23
- Age: 22
- Home club: Sydney FC

CHALLENGE
unique
Fun
ROLLERCOASTER
Continuous
Exciting
EVENTFUL
TOUGH
The Matildas on . . .
THE JOURNEY SO FAR IN ONE WORD
humbling
DEDICATED
INSPIRING
rewarding
adventure
CHALLENGING

SPOTLIGHT
Clare Wheeler

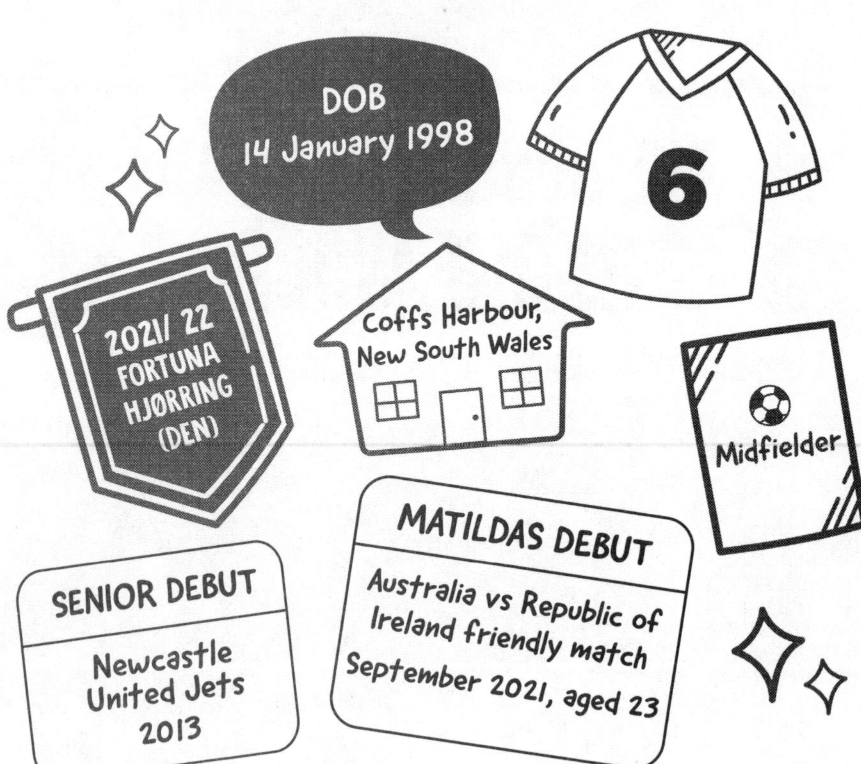
DOB
14 January 1998
6
2021/ 22
FORTUNA
HJØRRING
(DEN)
Coffs Harbour,
New South Wales
Midfielder
SENIOR DEBUT
Newcastle
United Jets
2013
MATILDAS DEBUT
Australia vs Republic of
Ireland friendly match
September 2021, aged 23

Clare Wheeler began playing football for her local club when she was ten years old, and she hasn't slowed down since! Three years after she first started playing, she was selected to join the Northern New South Wales squad in the State Youth League. Two years after that, she was selected for the Newcastle United Jets to make her W-League debut at fifteen.

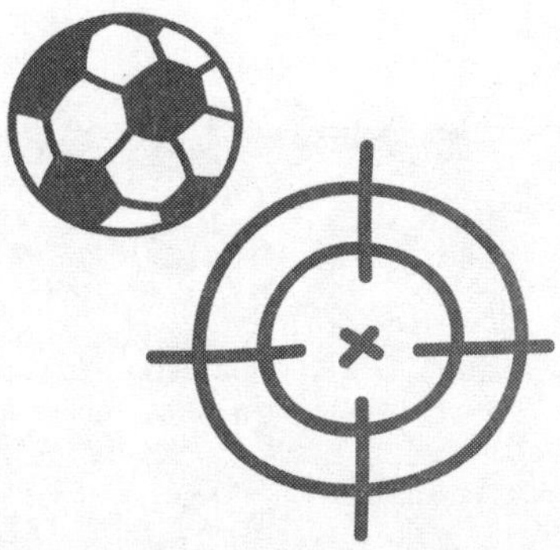

Then, in 2015, she started playing for the Young Matildas. A year later, she was captaining the squad. Clare's senior Matildas debut came in 2021, and she's played consistently since then.

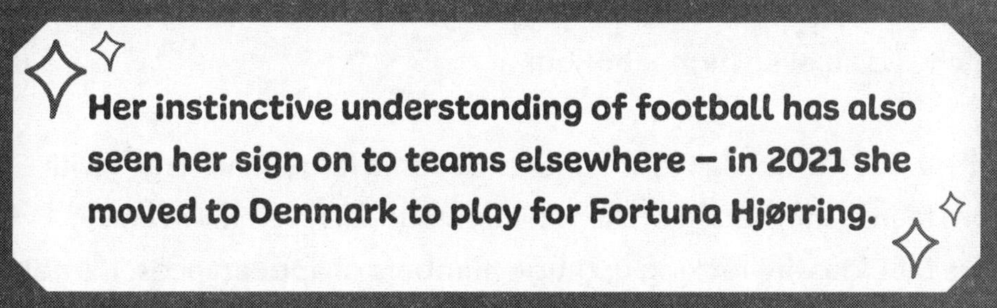

Her instinctive understanding of football has also seen her sign on to teams elsewhere – in 2021 she moved to Denmark to play for Fortuna Hjørring.

100-APPEARANCE FAMILY

When a Matilda steps onto the field and plays in their first international match for Australia they receive a cap number, their appearances then become tallied each time they play in a match – it means they've played in a game for their country (being called up to the squad but not appearing in the match is still an achievement, but doesn't quite count).

To receive a Matildas cap is a huge achievement. Players spend their footballing careers fighting for a chance to step on the field for the national team, even if it's just for a few minutes. To play in multiple matches is an even higher honour.

With women's football tournaments become larger and larger with more teams competing at the top international level, more and more Matildas are racking up huge numbers of appearances. It's not uncommon for players to rack up dozens of appearances over their international career. Even so, to make one hundred appearances for the Matildas is something very special.

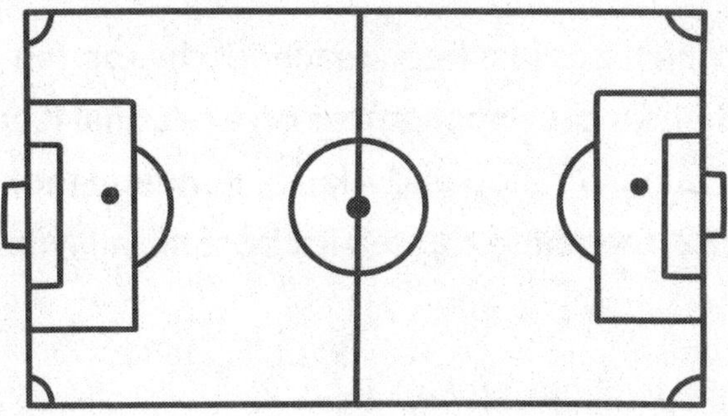

By the middle of 2022, fifteen players had played more than one hundred matches each for the Australian team. It's a massive achievement for Australian female players, noting the Socceroos only have two players with more than one hundred appearances. What's even more special is that most of those fifteen with more than one hundred appearances are still at the height of their careers, with plenty more to come!

The Australian player with the greatest number of appearances, male or female, is Cheryl Salisbury. She's been retired from the Matildas since 2009 but her 151-appearance record still stands. Lisa De Vanna, who retired from the national team in 2019, came the closest to the record at 150 appearances when she retired.

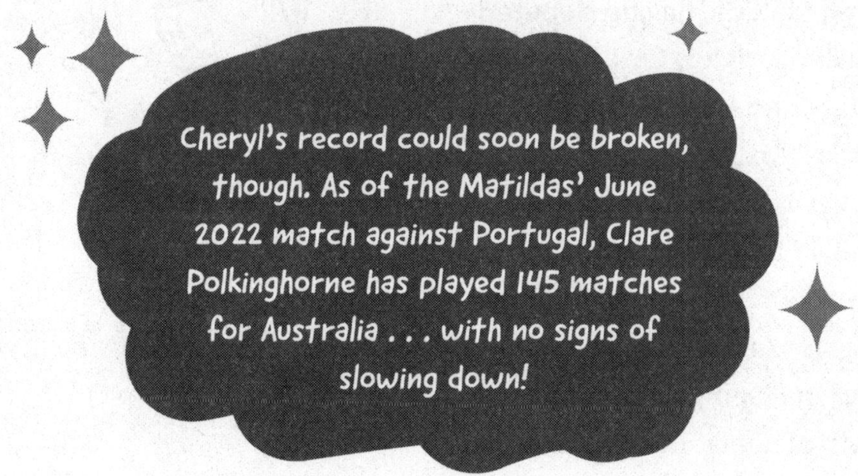

Another milestone that's just been reached: the top ten Australian footballers with the most appearances on a national team are all women! When Tameka Yallop and Alanna Kennedy took to the field in September 2022, the entire top-ten list became all women for the first time ever.

In June 2022, Lydia Williams became the first Matildas goalkeeper to reach one hundred appearances. She summed up the moment as the highlight of her career – even though playing any game for Australia is something to appreciate, the one hundredth game is special.

The current Matildas who have achieved one hundred appearances are some of the most senior on the team. Lydia Williams is currently the longest-serving Matilda, having debuted for Australia in July 2005, and she's been around for every current Matildas' first appearance. Despite her own massive achievement, she's said that the most amazing thing about playing one hundred games for Australia has been being part of the team, witnessing the growth of her teammates and getting to call them her friends.

THE MATILDAS' 100-APPEARANCES FAMILY (AS AT JULY 2022)

- Anissa Tann
  - Matilda from 1988–2002
  - Matildas debut: Australia vs Brazil; June 1988
  - 100th game: Australia vs USA; October 2002

- Cheryl Salisbury
  - Matilda from 1994–2009
  - Matildas debut: Australia vs Russia; April 1994
  - 100th game: Australia vs USA; August 2004

- Joanne Peters
  - Matilda from 1996–2009
  - Matildas debut: Australia vs New Zealand; March 1996
  - 100th game: Australia vs Taiwan; February 2007

- Heather Garriock
  - Matilda from 1999–2011
  - Matildas debut: Australia vs China; October 1999
  - 100th game: Australia vs USA; April 2008

- Lisa De Vanna
  - Matilda from 2004–2019
  - Matildas debut: Australia vs New Zealand; February 2004
  - 100th game: Australia vs USA; June 2015

- Lydia Williams
    - Matilda from 2005–present
    - Matildas debut: Australia vs South Korea; July 2005
    - 100th game: Australia vs Portugal; June 2022

- Clare Polkinghorne
    - Matilda from 2006–present
    - Matildas debut: Australia vs China; June 2006
    - 100th game: Australia vs Portugal; March 2018

- Elise Kellond-Knight
    - Matilda from 2007–present
    - Matildas debut: Australia vs Hong Kong; August 2007
    - 100th game: Australia vs England; October 2018

- Kyah Simon
    - Matilda from 2007–present
    - Matildas debut: Australia vs Hong Kong; August 2007
    - 100th game: Australia vs Sweden; August 2021

- Tameka Yallop
    - Matilda from 2007–present
    - Matildas debut: Australia vs Hong Kong; August 2007
    - 100th game: Australia vs USA; November 2021

- Samantha Kerr
    - Matilda from 2009–present
    - Matildas debut: Australia vs Italy; February 2009
    - 100th game: Australia vs Ireland; September 2021

- Emily van Egmond
    - Matilda from 2010–present
    - Matildas debut: Australia vs North Korea; March 2010
    - 100th game: Australia vs Denmark; June 2021

- Caitlin Foord
    - Matilda from 2011–present
    - Matildas debut: Australia vs New Zealand; May 2011
    - 100th game: Australia vs New Zealand; April 2022

- Alanna Kennedy
    - Matilda from 2012–present
    - Matildas debut: Australia vs New Zealand; June 2012
    - 100th game: Australia vs Brazil; October 2021

- Steph Catley
    - Matilda from 2012–present
    - Matildas debut: Australia vs New Zealand; June 2012
    - 100th game: Australia vs South Korea; January 2022

SPOTLIGHT

Teagan Micah

Teagan Micah has played football since she was seven, positioned in goal from an early age. She has a natural ability, which she's amplified by training and hard work to become a sought-after player for clubs in Australia, the USA and Sweden . . . and, of course, the Matildas.

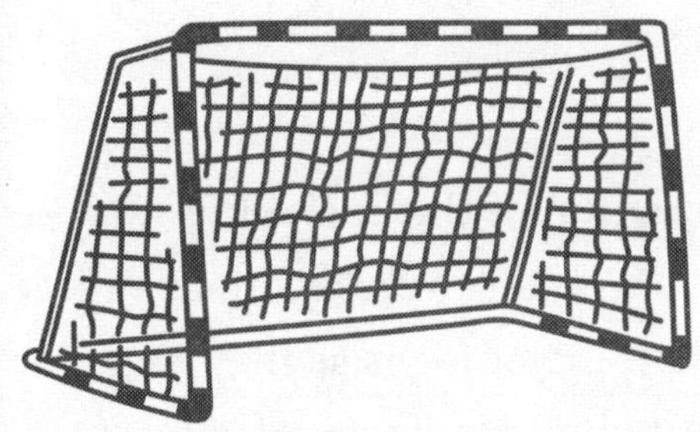

While Teagan didn't make her Matildas debut until 2021, she's travelled with the squad to a number of tournaments as a reserve goalkeeper since 2017. Teagan's played for clubs across Australia, as well as the USA, Norway and now Sweden, where she signed in 2021.

Within twelve months, she's played almost two dozen games for FC Rosengård. Despite her recent Matildas debut, she's also managed to rack up more than ten appearances already!

Looking forward to Australia and New Zealand **2023**

Following the 2022 AFC Women's Asian Cup, the Matildas were the twelfth ranked women's team in the world. They're also one of Australia's most-loved sporting teams.

Preparing for the upcoming FIFA Women's World Cup 2023™ is their major focus as they look to build on their previous performances as fourth-place holders in the 2020 Tokyo Olympics, and champions of the 2010 Asian Cup.

So far, the team have come together a few times since the 2022 Asian Cup, playing in friendly matches against New Zealand, Spain, Portugal and Canada.

Tony Gustavsson, the head coach, has used the friendlies to mix up the squad, giving minutes to some new and less-familiar players like Angela Beard, Jamilla Rankin, Rachel Lowe, Taylor Ray and Indiah-Paige Riley, who have only a handful of national team appearances between them. And players like Jacynta Galabadaarachchi, Mackenzie Hawkesby, Winonah Heatley and Matilda McNamara have yet to make their Matilda debuts – but they've all impressed the coaches enough to join the squad on one occasion or the other over the past eighteen months. Each of them have the potential to be part of the FIFA Women's World Cup 2023™ line-up.

While the friendlies haven't always gone the way the Matildas intended, the players are confident their World Cup campaign will be their best yet. Gustavsson's training motto is 'one day better'. Tie that in with the Matildas' 'Never Say Die' attitude, and you have the makings of a motivated team with a lot of belief in their ability to perform at a world-class level.

This positive attitude allowed the team to bounce back after a 0–7 loss in a friendly against Spain to draw 1–1 against Portugal in another match just three days later. As a squad missing its most experienced members, it was a proud moment for the team to be able to turn things around.

And as the Australian footballing community looks ahead to the next World Cup, they're also looking back and recognising the women pioneers who came before.

The incredible successes of the Matildas have always been against the odds. Even now, there are still fewer opportunities for women to play elite-level football consistently throughout the year than there are for men, and yet the Matildas are Australia's more successful football team.

But, with the Matildas' 'Never Say Die' spirit, fantastic track record and the incredible opportunities at their feet, the FIFA Women's World Cup 2023™ is going to be an epic tournament!

"WE'RE SO *excited* THAT WE GET TO GO OUT THERE AND DON THE *Green & Gold* JERSEY AT A *World Cup* IN FRONT OF *Home Fans*, WE'RE ALL BUZZING. I CAN'T WAIT."

— EMILY VAN EGMOND —

MATILDAS RECORDS

MOST GOALS

1. Sam Kerr (2009–present) – 59 goals
2. Lisa De Vanna (2004–2019) – 47 goals
3. Kate Gill (2004–2015) – 41 goals

MOST APPEARANCES

1. Cheryl Salisbury (1994–2009) – 151 games
2. Lisa De Vanna (2004–2019) – 150 games
3. Clare Polkinghorne (2006–present) – 146 games

MOST CLEAN SHEETS

1. Melissa Barbieri (2002–2015) – 34 clean sheets
2. Lydia Williams (2005–present) – 33 clean sheets
3. Tracey Wheeler (1989–2000) – 11 clean sheets
   Mackenzie Arnold (2012–present) – 11 clean sheets

LONGEST-SERVING

1. Lydia Williams (2005–present) – 17 years
2. Clare Polkinghorne (2006–present) – 16 years
3. Lisa De Vanna (2004–2019) – 15 years

CAPTAINS

- Julie Dolan, 1979–1984
- Sue Monteath, 1984–1987
- Julie Murray, 1995–1999
- Alison Forman, 2000
- Cheryl Salisbury, 2003–2009
- Melissa Barbieri, 2010–2013
- Clare Polkinghorne & Kate Gill, 2013–2014
- Clare Polkinghorne & Lisa De Vanna, 2015–2019
- Sam Kerr, 2019–present

TEAM HONOURS:

- OFC Women's Championship
    - Champions: 1994, 1998, 2003
    - Runners-up: 1983, 1986, 1991
- AFF Women's Championship
    - Champions: 2008
- AFC Women's Asian Cup
    - Champions: 2010
    - Runners-up: 2006, 2014, 2018

THE MATILDAS

- Julie Dolan
  - Cap #: 1
  - Debuted: 1979
- Shona Bass
  - Cap #: 2
  - Debuted: 1979
- Sandra Brentnall
  - Cap #: 3
  - Debuted: 1979
- Julie Clayton
  - Cap #: 4
  - Debuted: 1979
- Kim Coates
  - Cap #: 5
  - Debuted: 1979
- Cindy Heydon
  - Cap #: 6
  - Debuted: 1979
- Sharon Loveless
  - Cap #: 7
  - Debuted: 1979
- Toni McMahon
  - Cap #: 8
  - Debuted: 1979
- Sue Monteath
  - Cap #: 9
  - Debuted: 1979
- Rose Van Bruinessen
  - Cap #: 10
  - Debuted: 1979
- Leigh Wardell
  - Cap #: 11
  - Debuted: 1979
- Fiona McKenzie
  - Cap #: 12
  - Debuted: 1979
- Diana Hall
  - Cap #: 13
  - Debuted: 1979
- Judy Pettitt
  - Cap #: 14
  - Debuted: 1979
- Carla Grims
  - Cap #: 15
  - Debuted: 1979
- Jamie Rosman
  - Cap #: 16
  - Debuted: 1980
- Theresa Deas (Jones)
  - Cap #: 17
  - Debuted: 1980
- Kim Lembryk
  - Cap #: 18
  - Debuted: 1981

- Kerry Millman
    - Cap #: 19
    - Debuted: 1981
- Julie Porter
    - Cap #: 20
    - Debuted: 1981
- Leanne Priestly
    - Cap #: 21
    - Debuted: 1981
- Tracey Singleton
    - Cap #: 22
    - Debuted: 1981
- Leah Wright
    - Cap #: 23
    - Debuted: 1981
- Marie Russell
    - Cap #: 24
    - Debuted: 1981
- Sharon Wass
    - Cap #: 25
    - Debuted: 1981
- Renaye Iserief
    - Cap #: 26
    - Debuted: 1983
- Vicki Salmons
    - Cap #: 27
    - Debuted: 1983
- Kristen Theile
    - Cap #: 28
    - Debuted: 1983
- Joanne Millman
    - Cap #: 29
    - Debuted: 1983
- Karen Menzies
    - Cap #: 30
    - Debuted: 1983
- Margaret Petrov
    - Cap #: 31
    - Debuted: 1984
- Lisa Dunne
    - Cap #: 32
    - Debuted: 1984
- Mandi Langlar
    - Cap #: 33
    - Debuted: 1984
- Debra Bonshore
    - Cap #: 34
    - Debuted: 1984
- Kim Dunlop
    - Cap #: 35
    - Debuted: 1984
- Jane Oakley
    - Cap #: 36
    - Debuted: 1984
- Andrea Martin
    - Cap #: 37
    - Debuted: 1986
- Terri McQueen
    - Cap #: 38
    - Debuted: 1986

- Mariana Milanovic
    - Cap #: 39
    - Debuted: 1986
- Sabine Buschmann
    - Cap #: 40
    - Debuted: 1986
- Sue Buswell
    - Cap #: 41
    - Debuted: 1986
- Moya Dodd
    - Cap #: 42
    - Debuted: 1986
- Lisa Rader
    - Cap #: 43
    - Debuted: 1986
- Sharon Dewar
    - Cap #: 44
    - Debuted: 1987
- Janine McPhee
    - Cap #: 45
    - Debuted: 1987
- Michelle Sawyers
    - Cap #: 46
    - Debuted: 1987
- Lyn Spencer
    - Cap #: 47
    - Debuted: 1987
- Amanda George
    - Cap #: 48
    - Debuted: 1987
- Jill Latimer
    - Cap #: 49
    - Debuted: 1987
- Janelle Renshaw
    - Cap #: 50
    - Debuted: 1987
- Julie Murray
    - Cap #: 51
    - Debuted: 1987
- Debbie Nichols
    - Cap #: 52
    - Debuted: 1988
- Janine Riddington
    - Cap #: 53
    - Debuted: 1988
- Anissa Tann
    - Cap #: 54
    - Debuted: 1988
- Carol Vinson
    - Cap #: 55
    - Debuted: 1988
- Linda Hughes
    - Cap #: 56
    - Debuted: 1989
- Kristine James
    - Cap #: 57
    - Debuted: 1989
- Tracey Wheeler
    - Cap #: 58
    - Debuted: 1989

- Dalys Carmody
    - Cap #: 59
    - Debuted: 1989
- Karen Harris
    - Cap #: 60
    - Debuted: 1989
- Alison Forman
    - Cap #: 61
    - Debuted: 1989
- Carolyn Monk
    - Cap #: 62
    - Debuted: 1989
- Sonia Gegenhuber
    - Cap #: 63
    - Debuted: 1991
- Kaylene Janssen
    - Cap #: 64
    - Debuted: 1991
- Sharon Young
    - Cap #: 65
    - Debuted: 1991
- Angela Iannotta
    - Cap #: 66
    - Debuted: 1991
- Traci Bartlett
    - Cap #: 67
    - Debuted: 1991
- Sharon Black
    - Cap #: 68
    - Debuted: 1991
- Sarah Cooper
    - Cap #: 69
    - Debuted: 1991
- Donna Fredrickson
    - Cap #: 70
    - Debuted: 1991
- Tracey Jenkins
    - Cap #: 71
    - Debuted: 1991
- Jackie Hadden
    - Cap #: 72
    - Debuted: 1994
- Claire Nichols
    - Cap #: 73
    - Debuted: 1994
- Denie Pentecost
    - Cap #: 74
    - Debuted: 1994
- Cheryl Salisbury
    - Cap #: 75
    - Debuted: 1994
- Sacha Wainwright
    - Cap #: 76
    - Debuted: 1994
- Trena Youngblutt
    - Cap #: 77
    - Debuted: 1994
- Lizzy Claydon
    - Cap #: 78
    - Debuted: 1994

- Lisa Casagrande
    - Cap #: 79
    - Debuted: 1994
- Bridgette Starr
    - Cap #: 80
    - Debuted: 1994
- Amanda Paterson
    - Cap #: 81
    - Debuted: 1994
- Michelle Prouten
    - Cap #: 82
    - Debuted: 1994
- Michelle Watson
    - Cap #: 83
    - Debuted: 1994
- Karly Pumpa
    - Cap #: 84
    - Debuted: 1994
- Kim Revell
    - Cap #: 85
    - Debuted: 1995
- Justine Fisher
    - Cap #: 86
    - Debuted: 1995
- Louise McMurtrie
    - Cap #: 87
    - Debuted: 1995
- Denise Lofthouse
    - Cap #: 88
    - Debuted: 1995
- Di Alagich
    - Cap #: 89
    - Debuted: 1995
- Katrina Boyd
    - Cap #: 90
    - Debuted: 1996
- Joanne Peters
    - Cap #: 91
    - Debuted: 1996
- Kristyn Swaffer
    - Cap #: 92
    - Debuted: 1996
- Tammie Thornton
    - Cap #: 93
    - Debuted: 1996
- Amy Wilson
    - Cap #: 94
    - Debuted: 1996
- Shelley Youman
    - Cap #: 95
    - Debuted: 1996
- Bryony Duus
    - Cap #: 96
    - Debuted: 1996
- Kelly Golebiowski
    - Cap #: 97
    - Debuted: 1996
- Belinda Kitching
    - Cap #: 98
    - Debuted: 1996

- Amy Duggan
  - Cap #: 99
  - Debuted: 1997
- Kristy Moore
  - Cap #: 100
  - Debuted: 1997
- Alicia Ferguson
  - Cap #: 101
  - Debuted: 1997
- Tracie McGovern
  - Cap #: 102
  - Debuted: 1997
- Trudy Diamond
  - Cap #: 103
  - Debuted: 1997
- Natalie Thomas
  - Cap #: 104
  - Debuted: 1998
- Joanne Butland
  - Cap #: 105
  - Debuted: 1999
- Peita-Claire Hepperlin
  - Cap #: 106
  - Debuted: 1999
- Danielle Small
  - Cap #: 107
  - Debuted: 1999
- Heather Garriock
  - Cap #: 108
  - Debuted: 1999
- Leanne Trimboli
  - Cap #: 109
  - Debuted: 2000
- Kate McShea
  - Cap #: 110
  - Debuted: 2000
- April Mann
  - Cap #: 111
  - Debuted: 2001
- Taryn Rockall
  - Cap #: 112
  - Debuted: 2001
- Rhian Davies
  - Cap #: 113
  - Debuted: 2002
- Gillian Foster
  - Cap #: 114
  - Debuted: 2002
- Zoe Nolan
  - Cap #: 115
  - Debuted: 2002
- Cassandra Kell
  - Cap #: 116
  - Debuted: 2002
- Olivia Hohnke
  - Cap #: 117
  - Debuted: 2002
- Tal Karp
  - Cap #: 118
  - Debuted: 2002

- Thea Slatyer
    - Cap #: 119
    - Debuted: 2002
- Melissa Barbieri
    - Cap #: 120
    - Debuted: 2002
- Hayley Crawford
    - Cap #: 121
    - Debuted: 2003
- Pam Grant
    - Cap #: 122
    - Debuted: 2003
- Karla Reuter
    - Cap #: 123
    - Debuted: 2003
- Lisa De Vanna
    - Cap #: 124
    - Debuted: 2004
- Sarah Walsh
    - Cap #: 125
    - Debuted: 2004
- Leah Blayney
    - Cap #: 126
    - Debuted: 2004
- Kate Gill
    - Cap #: 127
    - Debuted: 2004
- Lana Harch
    - Cap #: 128
    - Debuted: 2004
- Selin Kuralay
    - Cap #: 129
    - Debuted: 2004
- Kylie Ledbrook
    - Cap #: 130
    - Debuted: 2004
- Sally Shipard
    - Cap #: 131
    - Debuted: 2004
- Collette McCallum
    - Cap #: 132
    - Debuted: 2005
- Kim Carroll
    - Cap #: 133
    - Debuted: 2005
- Caitlin Munoz
    - Cap #: 134
    - Debuted: 2005
- Jessica Mitchell
    - Cap #: 135
    - Debuted: 2005
- Emma Wirkus
    - Cap #: 136
    - Debuted: 2005
- Joanne Burgess
    - Cap #: 137
    - Debuted: 2005
- Lydia Williams
    - Cap #: 138
    - Debuted: 2005

- Lauren Colthorpe
  - Cap #: 139
  - Debuted: 2005
- Clare Polkinghorne
  - Cap #: 140
  - Debuted: 2006
- Sasha McDonell
  - Cap #: 141
  - Debuted: 2006
- Amber Neilson
  - Cap #: 142
  - Debuted: 2006
- Jenna Tristram
  - Cap #: 143
  - Debuted: 2007
- Ellen Beaumont
  - Cap #: 144
  - Debuted: 2007
- Louisa Bisby
  - Cap #: 145
  - Debuted: 2007
- Amy Chapman
  - Cap #: 146
  - Debuted: 2007
- Victoria Balomenos
  - Cap #: 147
  - Debuted: 2007
- Tameka Yallop
  - Cap #: 148
  - Debuted: 2007
- Caitlin Cooper
  - Cap #: 149
  - Debuted: 2007
- Rachel Cooper
  - Cap #: 150
  - Debuted: 2007
- Rachael Doyle
  - Cap #: 151
  - Debuted: 2007
- Lyndsay Glohe
  - Cap #: 152
  - Debuted: 2007
- Elise Kellond-Knight
  - Cap #: 153
  - Debuted: 2007
- Ellyse Perry
  - Cap #: 154
  - Debuted: 2007
- Teresa Polias
  - Cap #: 155
  - Debuted: 2007
- Renee Rollason
  - Cap #: 156
  - Debuted: 2007
- Kyah Simon
  - Cap #: 157
  - Debuted: 2007
- Grace Gill-McGrath
  - Cap #: 158
  - Debuted: 2007

- Jenna Kingsley
    - Cap #: 159
    - Debuted: 2007
- Brooke Spence
    - Cap #: 160
    - Debuted: 2008
- Ella Mastrantonio
    - Cap #: 161
    - Debuted: 2008
- Servet Uzunlar
    - Cap #: 162
    - Debuted: 2008
- Leena Khamis
    - Cap #: 163
    - Debuted: 2008
- Ashleigh Sykes
    - Cap #: 164
    - Debuted: 2008
- Christine Walters
    - Cap #: 165
    - Debuted: 2008
- Danielle Brogan
    - Cap #: 166
    - Debuted: 2009
- Ellie Brush
    - Cap #: 167
    - Debuted: 2009
- Sam Kerr
    - Cap #: 168
    - Debuted: 2009
- Aivi Luik
    - Cap #: 169
    - Debuted: 2010
- Michelle Heyman
    - Cap #: 170
    - Debuted: 2010
- Laura Brock
    - Cap #: 171
    - Debuted: 2010
- Emily van Egmond
    - Cap #: 172
    - Debuted: 2010
- Teigen Allen
    - Cap #: 173
    - Debuted: 2010
- Catherine Cannuli
    - Cap #: 174
    - Debuted: 2011
- Caitlin Foord
    - Cap #: 175
    - Debuted: 2011
- Ash Brown
    - Cap #: 176
    - Debuted: 2012
- Steph Catley
    - Cap #: 177
    - Debuted: 2012
- Alanna Kennedy
    - Cap #: 178
    - Debuted: 2012

- Hayley Raso
  - Cap #: 179
  - Debuted: 2012
- Georgia Yeoman-Dale
  - Cap #: 180
  - Debuted: 2012
- Nicola Bolger
  - Cap #: 181
  - Debuted: 2012
- Emily Gielnik
  - Cap #: 182
  - Debuted: 2012
- Katrina Gorry
  - Cap #: 183
  - Debuted: 2012
- Brianna Davey
  - Cap #: 184
  - Debuted: 2012
- Mackenzie Arnold
  - Cap #: 185
  - Debuted: 2012
- Emma Checker
  - Cap #: 186
  - Debuted: 2012
- Vedrana Popovic
  - Cap #: 187
  - Debuted: 2013
- Chloe Logarzo
  - Cap #: 188
  - Debuted: 2013
- Hannah Brewer
  - Cap #: 189
  - Debuted: 2014
- Gema Simon
  - Cap #: 190
  - Debuted: 2014
- Rhali Dobson
  - Cap #: 191
  - Debuted: 2014
- Larissa Crummer
  - Cap #: 192
  - Debuted: 2015
- Casey Dumont
  - Cap #: 193
  - Debuted: 2015
- Amy Harrison
  - Cap #: 194
  - Debuted: 2015
- Alex Chidiac
  - Cap #: 195
  - Debuted: 2015
- Tara Andrews
  - Cap #: 196
  - Debuted: 2015
- Ellie Carpenter
  - Cap #: 197
  - Debuted: 2016
- Princess Ibini
  - Cap #: 198
  - Debuted: 2017

- Eliza Campbell
  - Cap #: 199
  - Debuted: 2017
- Emily Condon
  - Cap #: 200
  - Debuted: 2018
- Rachel Lowe
  - Cap #: 201
  - Debuted: 2018
- Mary Fowler
  - Cap #: 202
  - Debuted: 2018
- Amy Sayer
  - Cap #: 203
  - Debuted: 2018
- Karly Roestbakken
  - Cap #: 204
  - Debuted: 2019
- Jenna McCormick
  - Cap #: 205
  - Debuted: 2019
- Beatrice Goad
  - Cap #: 206
  - Debuted: 2021
- Indiah-Paige Riley
  - Cap #: 207
  - Debuted: 2021
- Alex Huynh
  - Cap #: 208
  - Debuted: 2021
- Dylan Holmes
  - Cap #: 209
  - Debuted: 2021
- Kyra Cooney-Cross
  - Cap #: 210
  - Debuted: 2021
- Courtney Nevin
  - Cap #: 211
  - Debuted: 2021
- Teagan Micah
  - Cap #: 212
  - Debuted: 2021
- Clare Wheeler
  - Cap #: 213
  - Debuted: 2021
- Charlotte Grant
  - Cap #: 214
  - Debuted: 2021
- Angela Beard
  - Cap #: 215
  - Debuted: 2021
- Remy Siemsen
  - Cap #: 216
  - Debuted: 2021
- Bryleeh Henry
  - Cap #: 217
  - Debuted: 2021
- Jessika Nash
  - Cap #: 218
  - Debuted: 2021

- Holly McNamara
  - Cap #: 219
  - Debuted: 2022
- Cortnee Vine
  - Cap #: 220
  - Debuted: 2022
- Jamilla Rankin
  - Cap #: 221
  - Debuted: 2022
- Taylor Ray
  - Cap #: 222
  - Debuted: 2022

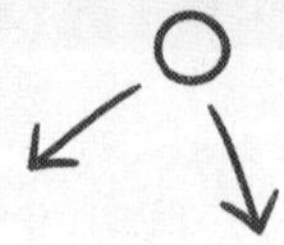

Journey to 2023

Player spotlights

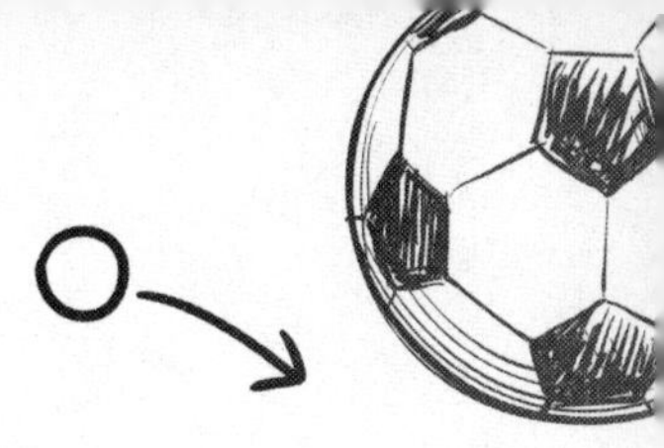

What makes a Matilda

Put it into practice

FOLLOW THE
COMMBANK MATILDAS

matildas.com.au

matildas

matildas

TheMatildas

footballaustralia